T0065159

My Success in America

GEORGE WELCEL

ARCHWAY PUBLISHING

Copyright © 2023 George Welcel.

All rights reserved. No part of this book may be used or reproduced by any means, graphic, electronic, or mechanical, including photocopying, recording, taping or by any information storage retrieval system without the written permission of the author except in the case of brief quotations embodied in critical articles and reviews.

This book is a work of non-fiction. Unless otherwise noted, the author and the publisher make no explicit guarantees as to the accuracy of the information contained in this book and in some cases, names of people and places have been altered to protect their privacy.

Archway Publishing books may be ordered through booksellers or by contacting:

Archway Publishing
1663 Liberty Drive
Bloomington, IN 47403
www.archwaypublishing.com
844-669-3957

Because of the dynamic nature of the Internet, any web addresses or links contained in this book may have changed since publication and may no longer be valid. The views expressed in this work are solely those of the author and do not necessarily reflect the views of the publisher, and the publisher hereby disclaims any responsibility for them.

Any people depicted in stock imagery provided by Getty Images are models, and such images are being used for illustrative purposes only. Certain stock imagery © Getty Images.

ISBN: 978-1-6657-4144-6 (sc)
ISBN: 978-1-6657-4229-0 (hc)
ISBN: 978-1-6657-4145-3 (e)

Library of Congress Control Number: 2023905729

Print information available on the last page.

Archway Publishing rev. date: 04/28/2023

CONTENTS

INTRODUCTION

It's been almost thirty years since this biographical book, *Mój sukces w Ameryce* (My success in America), was written. After this amount of time, I have decided to have it translated into English. I have been living in the USA for forty-six years, and I lived under Communism for thirty years of my youth. We were then called the *bananowa młodzież* (young bloods. Currently in the United States, so-called left-wing democracy is coming to prominence. Young people do not know what socialism or communism are. This made me decide to have this book translated into English to show them what living under Communism was like. I have also seen and written about what is wrong in America.

I am a conservative and I supported Donald Trump in the 2016 election; I even received a letter of thanks from him. Currently I live on my ranch in Masuria, Poland, although my business of building 120 condominiums in Florida still keeps me there, so I live here and there.

I recommend my book to all the people who want to know what socialism was like and who want to help the right wing restore the former glory of the United States of America.

To my mother, Kazia Dębska, whom I could always count on. When I started this book, She lived happily, and when I finished, I was overwhelmed by her tragic death.

CHAPTER 1

IN COMMUNIST POLAND

★ ★ ★

I did not know my father. However, I know that he still had the noble name of Welcel vel Dubio on his ID. He was last seen in a uniform with a machine gun in the Old Town. I know that he fought in the Warsaw Uprising, fell into enemy hands, and died in Oświęcim. The Germans took my mother to Chemnitz, and even though she was pregnant, she was forced to work in a weapons factory. It was there, during an American air raid in a basement that served as a shelter, that I was born. It was on March 4, 1945, when the Reich, increasingly poorly supplied with food, surrounded by the tight ring of the Allied forces and constantly bombed, seemed to be the worst place on earth for a woman with a baby—and even more so for a Polish woman and a forced laborer—or, rather, a slave.

I know from my mother that the Germans there treated her humanely and with some respect, regardless of the newborn child. They brought food and a variety of clothes that she used to make diapers for me. But despite their kindness, it was very difficult for her.

After the Americans entered Chemnitz, my mother, as a young and attractive woman, had many offers to go to the States. However, her parents stayed in Warsaw, so her heart dictated her decision to return.

It was suggested that when writing these memoirs I should skip the years I spent in the People's Republic of Poland. Those times no longer interest the reader, who is weary of martyrdom literature and not eager to settle accounts with the latest history. So if, contrary to these arguments, I am writing about Communist Poland, I am doing so for two reasons. Firstly, as a man who has lived in the United States of America for many years, and thus is able to compare the two regimes, I have a slightly different view of Communism than the typical "martyrdom" view. Secondly, without taking into account the political and economic background, the story of my emigration would be incomplete. After all, there are economic reasons for my departure from economics, and the politics and economy of the Polish People's Republic to a large extent shaped the baggage of experiences I stood in possession of on American soil.

My situation in the Polish People's Republic was quite special because my mother and grandfather belonged to the so-called private initiative. My family's mercantile traditions went back to the interwar period, which would have been a plus for them in any normal country. In Communist Poland, businessmen, contemptuously called "privateers," were a kind of accursed caste. For ideological reasons, they were persecuted fiscally and administratively, and as if that were not enough, the odium fell on their children as well. Such an entry was in the People's Republic of Poland, especially in Stalinist times, as a stigma. What is worse, it developed a reluctant attitude toward people who, thanks to their ingenuity and work, achieved above-average property status. On the one hand, this was the result of propaganda constantly attacking wealthy merchants, craftsmen, and peasants; and on the other, the result of social envy, which was especially strong in the situation of general poverty. The Communists, by destroying private entrepreneurship, were implementing Mayakovsky's gloomy slogan: "the individual is nothing, the individual is zero." Only the masses were to count—the working masses of towns and villages—along with their alleged representative and guiding force, the party.

I am a bit afraid that although the party is no more, the specter of aversion toward wealthy people has survived in the society to this day. Like many other remnants of Communism, it is possible to cure this, but it will take time.

Unfortunately the tenement house in which my mother lived before the uprising was no longer there, and the beautiful house of my grandparents in Legionowo was forcibly inhabited by tenants. Immediately after the war, my grandparents lived in their six-apartment house in Legionowo, where there was a beautiful old garden.

Grandfather grew good, sweet strawberries as a hobby. The house had no sewage system, and people used to go to the toilet in a small house in the garden. There is a funny story connected with it; one morning my grandfather came back from the toilet and said, "You know what I'm going to tell you? Someone stole your shit from the toilet last night!" The local stalkers had probably pumped it out at night. If they had asked me, I would have given it to them for free.

Everyone laughed at this. It was repeated as a joke over the years. Later we had to settle down in Praga, in a one-room flat without any comforts. There were four of us: me, my sister, my mother, and her second husband. And the Communist system, in its most dangerous, Stalinist version, was slowly but consistently being installed all around.

But my family were tough people who did not give up easily. Grandfather Ignacy, who was my father's replacement, had two wholesale and retail stores at Plac Kercelego in Warsaw's Wola district before the war. After the war, which destroyed the shops and all his belongings, he had to start all over again and opened the so-called double booth in Praga, where he traded in toys and devotional religious articles, the latter of which particularly irritated the Communist authorities. The trade in devotional articles was quickly forbidden, and soon after that, the entire shopping area (i.e., the popular Zieleniak, named after Zieleniecka Street) was closed. he received a point in Targówek. There, however, the trade was much worse, and subsequent applications for a better location were refused.

There was no other option, so my grandparents moved the business to their apartment. Needless to say, in the light of the restrictive regulations of that time, it was illegal, similar to having a foreign currency, employing too many employees, and so forth. This gloomy paranoia seems to be forgotten by all those who want to see the PRL as a normal reality today, perhaps most heavily burdened with certain errors.

The People's Republic of Poland conducted a police search in the apartment of my neighbor, an old woman, and confiscated evidence of a crime—a few pieces of lard and a few gold coins! It was 1955 and that was the "normal reality" I had to grow up in.

As I have already mentioned, our apartment was located in Praga, a district that was not one of the safest. It can be said that I grew up in a reality quite similar to those described by Stanisław Grzesiuk in the once widely read book *Boso ale w ostrogach* (bandit inclinations), but in many respects he was the proverbial boy of Praga—the one who will not sell cheap leather in a street fight and will not be afraid of just anything.

My first Praga memory is about proving my courage. I was six years old when our tenement house was renovated and the ladder scaffolding reached up to the fourth floor. I started at night to climb it higher and higher.

A little later, I started "training with trams"—that is, jumping in and out of them while running. I started at low speeds to gradually master the technique. When I decided that I was already good, I risked a real stunt jump. I remember that the tram was going very fast along Stalowa Street, which was paved with cobblestones. I landed on the stones face-first; then, out of pain and fear, I jumped up and fell into the nearest gate.

I crouched somewhere in a corner and, like a wounded animal, I wanted to bury myself in the burrow to be alone. But I couldn't be alone, because of course there was a great sensation, and people started gathering around me. They said something, but the words didn't reach me at all. Finally I somehow pushed my way through the crowd and ran home. Owing to a deep wound to my mouth and cheeks, I was all bloody. It is easy to imagine how my mother reacted.

For the sake of balance, I must mention that in those days, by accident or intuition, I also did something useful. Namely, I planted a tree in the yard. When visiting this place in 1993, I noticed with satisfaction that although there is no garden, my tree was handsome, reaching the roof of a four-story tenement house.

In general, I was a rascal, constantly causing educational problems but possessing a positive curiosity toward learning. I was reading based on pictures, and I wanted to go to school. I went to primary school a year earlier, but I did not have any special successes there. I think that is largely because there was no one to look after me properly, as my mother was absorbed in business most of the time. My grandfather—about whom I must say a few words, as he was the most important person for me in my childhood, next to my mother—tried to discipline me.

My grandfather's name was Ignacy Welcel. The surname proves that the family comes from Austria. In his youth, he stayed in tsarist Russia, where he graduated from a high-level gymnasium. He spoke Russian, however, he did so reluctantly, reserving the language mainly for curses. The most virulent Russian insults were uttered through grandfather's lips during a broadcast on Radio London and were addressed to communists. He was big, strong, and handsome for his age, with gray hair and a mustache. He was already suffering from arthritis and was walking with a cane, but he was a hard worker. In the face of harassment from the authorities, he was engaged in trade, paying the Communists horrendous, unfair so-called measuring taxes.

His wife, Grandmother Józia, née Wysocka, was a tall woman, of a strong, massive build. They lived together for half a century and had a harmonious marriage. Grandma made sure that the family did not lack anything, especially food. People feared having a house, car, or other so-called external signs of wealth because of the draconian Communist measures, so they bought food because the authorities did not scrutinize it. Family celebrations at my grandparents' house were therefore sumptuous, with the participation of several dozen people and often lasting three days.

I was thirteen when I finished elementary school, and I didn't quite know what to do with myself. The teacher who had led my class for the previous five years convinced my mother that I did not qualify for high school, technical college, or college. So, following most of my colleagues, I went to the basic vocational school in Annopol, Targówek, where, as one of the youngest students, I started a three-year education in an electrotechnics class.

At about the same time, I signed up in secret from my mother and grandfather to KS Polonia for boxing. I trained without head covers, as they were not for novices, and a few years later a specialist found that I had suffered a broken nose in the past. I was surprised that the injury had escaped my attention. When I look at the busts of famous Romans, I laugh at the thought that I have a noble, neat nose like them.

I would be lying if I said that I used my boxing skills only in the ring.

In the Polonia hall on Foksal Street, apart from training, there were also various events, including the New Year's Eve ball, which I went to in the company of Janusz, my club friend and a typical boy from Praga. I remember that the event started with a balloon, which my companion decided to take off of the basket it was attached to, and he climbed onto a table for that purpose. The gentlemen who sat at this table did not like it, and words quickly turned to deeds. They tried to hit us with champagne bottles. I hit so quickly that my opponent covered himself with his legs, and my friend Janusz did the same. In this way, New Year's Eve ended prematurely, and we happily disappeared before the arrival of the militia.

In two days, we had training in that room, and I showed Janusz bloodstains on the wall. It was the blood of our opponents—clear proof of the triumph. Janusz and I exchanged smiles silently. Our coach had no right to know anything about it. As a sixteen-year-old, I was a promising boxer. However, I had problems with my teeth, and there was a risk that I would not be allowed to participate in my first fight, the so-called first boxing step. Within a week, I had to have all my cavities tended to, which the dentist I went to found impossible. Then I asked to have my afflicted teeth extracted. I was sixteen, and this first fight in my life was my overriding goal. Today I would probably think longer about such a radical decision.

I remember that it was difficult because the tooth was firmly in my gums, so I even offered to help; telling the dentist that if we grabbed the pliers together it should be easier. She took offense, but I think I cheered her on, because right away, pushing her knee into my shoulder, she plucked out half a tooth with a crack in it, and a moment later the rest.

My "first boxing step" took place in Hala Gwardii. The first opponent, Burzynski, left the ring bleeding, and the next one gave up the fight by forfeit.

In this way, I won the Warsaw junior middleweight championship, and only then did I reveal to my family that I was a boxer. Grandpa was proud of me.

My boxing career did not last too long. My last fight was against Gwardia Białystok. Due to the lack of a middleweight player, the coach, Komuda, put me up against the Polish champion, Waluk. The first round was a draw, but in the second round I scored a series of punches and the coach threw a towel into the ring. On the way back from Białystok, I decided to stop boxing. The club was reluctant to accept this, and the president himself visited me in my apartment, but my mother explained to him that I was getting ready to study in a technical college and that I would not have time for training.

I wasn't an ace in my vocational school, but I didn't have any problems with my studies either. It all depended on whether I wanted to apply myself to a given subject. After the second grade, as a scout, I went to a summer camp in Masuria. The program included compulsory picking of the Colorado beetle, as well as work on the local state farm. Instead, the state-owned farms and my friend started to sneak out quietly for hitchhiking trips to Olsztyn.

On one occasion, two young educators tracked us down. Surprisingly, instead of scolding us, they suggested a walk into the forest. We were a bit surprised but felt nothing was wrong. The four of us went, and we were speaking normally when all of a sudden my friend received a kick from one of the teachers, and the other was readying to beat me. This is the way the thugs planned to punish us in the forest—a lynching without witnesses.

I started to run away, but I think the tutor wanted to get me, because he was chasing me through the brushwood. Luckily, the Elbląg Canal was on my way. Without thinking, I jumped into the water and swam to the other side. The teacher didn't want to make a fool of himself and didn't follow me. I avoided being beaten this way, but at school he gave me a low behavior rating.

I remember the blue jean craze, during which one could buy jeans on the so called "clothes bazaar" for a thousand zlote. Michał Burana and Tarnowski gave rock concerts in the Congress Hall, in the sixties, and it was there that I went on my first date.

But throughout my carefree life in the People's Republic of Poland, the reality of the Polish People's Republic was often a gloomy shadow. I remember how six men from the militia and the tax office came to our apartment. At seven in the morning, I was awakened by a pounding on the door.

Mom opened the door, and they rushed in unceremoniously. Their attitude toward the provision requiring the submission of a formal search warrant was more or less the same as during the occupation by the Gestapo.

I was lying barely awake on the couch when a series of questions came at me. They were interested in whom I was bringing the goods from and who was producing the devotional materials. I replied that I was studying in an electrical technical college and I was not involved in the company's matters. At that time, goods worth several hundred thousand zlote were confiscated, and my grandparents' apartment was sealed. I had hidden two packets of banknotes containing two hundred thousand each in the oven. They were not found during the search and thus survived this legal robbery in broad daylight. My grandparents and mother were taken to the police station for questioning.

In the evening, during a family meeting, my grandfather was wondering how to take two packages of twenty-dollar gold pieces and gold rubles (known as "pigs") from the sealed flat. Hidden on the balcony behind the windowsill, they had escaped the police's attention, but tomorrow's search would probably be more detailed.

I said that I could go to the balcony from my neighbor's balcony. I would have to jump or take a very long step to do this. Grandpa was scared, as it was high, and he did not want to agree, but I insisted. With four floors of space below me, under the cover of night, I jumped over to our balcony and took that gold out from under the windowsill. Of course, I had to go back the same way, because the front door was sealed with a wide official tape.

While still alive, my grandfather received an additional fine of 1,250,000 zlote, which he repaid and overpaid. High surcharges were an effective weapon of the Communist authorities to eliminate private initiatives. A craftsman who made a little money was immediately hit with excess surcharges so that he would not accidentally become a capitalist.

On top of that, my grandfather overpaid tens of thousands of zlote, but they did not want to return the surplus. This sum was regained by my mother only after my grandfather's death for the funeral costs.

After completing ZSZ, my mother asked whether I wanted to continue studying at the electrical technical college. I replied that I wanted to be independent, go to work, and earn money. So it happened. I got a job as an electrical technician trainee at Zakłady Dymitrów in Gocławska Street in Grochów. In those Communist times, where economic planning was central, there were no problems with getting a job. The salaries, on the other hand, were so low that workers could afford only a miserable existence.

We installed small transformers in Dymitrów. I applied myself diligently to my work, but still, something more was expected. After assembling the core sheets and windings, I moved the heavy, ready-made transformers by hand to the porcelain base. I was the youngest in the five man brigade and had to do the toughest, stupidest jobs. Somewhere in the middle of the day, sweat was running down my spine when a foreman named Wróbel started urging me to work faster. Maybe that's why I have had an aversion to excessive haste at work all my life. My brigade was paid bonuses for overproduction, but I was on an internship, earning a fixed salary of 500 zlote a month.

After a month of work, I bought an American jacket on my

clothes bazaar for exactly my entire monthly salary. My mother asked me again if I wanted to go to the technical school to continue my studies while there was still time. This time I gladly agreed, because I saw no future in this factory.

My mother had a friend of the director of the Kasprzaka on Okopowa Street in Wola, and he put me there. I started my second grade after a three-year vocational training, so I was practically two years behind. I was already one of the oldest in classes. I entered the classroom during a technical drawing session, and the teacher told me to sit at the last desk. I listened to the lecture in silence as balls of paper thrown by pranksters fell on me. I pretended to be cold blooded, not reacting to it.

When the lesson was over, we all went out into the field for a physical education lesson. Being friendly by nature, but with reservations toward strangers, I approached a group of boys from my class. All at once, the whole crowd pounced on me, knocking me down onto the grass. The oldest one began to press grass into my mouth. When I got up after a while, the biggest one said that the tradition of this class was that the newcomers eat grass. I punched the guy and gained the respect of the whole class. This man later became my best friend.

Technical School Konarski was famous for its high level of education. I slowly started to get used to systematic learning. At the end of the year, I was faced with two insufficient scores in geography and Russian. I always had big ambitions, so I stood up "on my head" to improve these subjects. I made it, passed to the third grade, and was pleased with myself.

Third grade classes were held in the afternoon. As future electricians, we put plastic washers under the fuses so that there was no light and the classes were temporarily suspended. After the lessons, we closed the classroom with a bolt, and the casino started. We were playing a game called bet.

A historian, a man of great stature, lived in the dormitory in the neighboring building. He was probably attracted by the light in our classroom, and using the scaffolding, he climbed up to the second floor and went inside. He saw several tables taken up by players and money on the tables.

I lived a carefree, happy, irresponsible life until the third grade of the electrical technical college, when I was expelled from school permanently. I had an F in Russian, but my other grades were good. The reason for my expulsion was organizing the casino, playing cards for money, and other matters, such as counterfeiting grades with a decoy. The headmaster cried, "The head must be broken off the hydra," although I was not the only one to blame.

For two weeks, I went to various electrical technical schools in Warsaw, seeking admission. I was very angry and disappointed when I was met with the answer "We don't need bullies." I didn't think of myself as a bully; I thought then that the world was unfair. Then I realized that you need to have a different, more responsible attitude toward life.

Finally, I was accepted into an electrical technical school on Nowogrodzka Street in Śródmieście. The late director Gajewski gave me a chance, for which I am grateful. In the fourth grade, I was even on the school council, responsible for matters of order. In the fifth grade, I played in the school theater as Prince Józef Sułkowski, Napoleon's adjutant. The dean of the theater school, Mr. Kreczmar, handed me a bouquet of carnations. A completely strange thing happened to me: the best student from the technical school, Mietek, made friends with me, and under his influence, I became a good student. He was impressed with my strength acquired in a bodybuilding club, Hercules, and my boxing skills from the Polonia club, and I liked his diligence in learning.

The teachers always said, "George is gifted if he only wants to be." And finally I wanted to be. I wanted to achieve something, be somebody, and see how other people lived.

After my grandparents died, I practically lived alone in the apartment where I grew up. For a sixteen-year-old boy, having his apartment was something to be envied. By eight in the morning, I would have a group of truants from my class there. They would bring wine, and we would play cards. This is how I enjoyed my apartment for about six months, until I got the eviction order.

When my grandparents were alive, no one dared to bring up the topic of registering me in the administration office in the event of their death. When the day of eviction came, we took all the furniture out of the apartment, and I moved in with my mother. Four men came to make a forced removal. They took only one broken chair out of the apartment into the corridor, and the eviction bill was 1,500 zlote. Of course, it was bullshit, and my mom never paid. I was never able to donate the apartment I was brought up in to the Communists. I found it regrettable that it was seen as moral for a grown-up boy to move into one medium-sized room with a married couple. The close quarters, embarrassment, and the complete lack of learning conditions haunted me throughout all the years of my studies. Therefore, at the end of my studies, I rented rooms from strangers.

A few years later, when, after various transitions and frequent school changes, I graduated from high school and passed to the university (Warsaw University of Technology), I decided that I would do business myself and relieve my mother a little. Earlier, I had traded Persian kilims in the villages with Mietek's help, so I had some experience. The first car I bought with my own money was a shiny, black ten-year-old English limousine from Humber.

I proposed to my mother that I would procure for her some sacred paintings, which she was selling. At first she did not want to agree. She said that it was a dangerous job, that I should study, and that I didn't need to be involved in it at all.

As I insisted, she eventually went with me to Częstochowa, and there she introduced me to the right people. After consultations and calculations, I hired a few families who had been involved in the production of religious pictures for a long time, and I brought the finished goods to my mother in Warsaw.

In the beginning, I was traveling by train. I liked these rides in the restaurant car over a nice dinner. Later, when I had a car, I was able to take to my employees from Częstochowa more photo paper and transport the final product more conveniently. Someone might ask why I did not buy paper in Czestochowa. Sure, it would have been easier, but I operated in the socialist economy, and the photo paper was available only in the capital.

The journeys from Warsaw to Częstochowa and back were generally full of adventures and dangers. After all, the militia could detain me under any pretext, such as a road check, and search the car. And as I mentioned before, the production of devotional items and trading in them by private persons were forbidden in the People's Republic of Poland. To protect myself, I had a simple idea: I inserted the broken end of a key into the trunk lock. When the policemen demanded that I open the trunk, I indicated with the greatest helplessness the defect that made it impossible to comply with the order. At home, I easily pulled out the broken key with tweezers.

One day, returning from Częstochowa on a snowy winter evening with a trunk full of goods, I suddenly saw a police car's flashing lights in my mirror. They called to me to stop, and I, aware of how much I could lose in a possible search, immediately decided to run away. At that time, I was a rally driver with a so-called 1-R license, and my new acquisition, a Fiat 125P, had wide American Goodyear tires. Under these circumstances, the policemen who were chasing me did not have much of a chance. I slowed down in next city to the prescribed 50 km/h, and then they got me.

They charged me for speeding but not ask to open the trunk. I explained that I was a rally driver and that this was my normal driving style. I ended up being referred to court, where I had to pay a 1,500 zlote fine. I consider it a success that by breaking the road traffic regulations, I drew their attention away from the most important thing—the contents of the trunk.

For six years I had successfully reconciled my difficult and, as you can see, not always safe business with my studies at the University of Technology. At twenty years old, my dream was to build electric cars. I ended up in an electrical department with a specialization in electric trains. In general, I must say that, unlike high school, where I had problems all the time, mainly for so-called educational reasons, my studies were going well. I became particularly emotional about the entrance examination when I found out about a transaction between my mother and a certain assistant who was willing to bribe me to become a student.

"I do not want to study for money," I stated emphatically to my mother, threatening that in such a situation I would not take the exams at all.

Mom gave up further talks with the assistant, and I passed with an average grade of B. The assistant, however, did not give up. He called my mother, saying that I had passed with a C+ and that in this situation his intervention was necessary. This lie, of course, had short legs, and he did not get a broken penny from my mother.

Of course, the period of the strikes sticks in my mind the most from my six years of study. In 1968, I was in my second year of the Warsaw University of Technology. Student strikes broke out all over Poland. The first occurred at the University of Warsaw. The immediate reason was a photo from the stage of the theater play *Dziady*, by Adam Mickiewicz. In one of the scenes, the actor exclaims, according to the original text, "to the Muscovite, to the Muscovite," and the audience applauded greatly at this moment. At that time, representatives of the Soviet Embassy were in the audience. The actors' anti-Russian accents were not welcome, and following that day, *Dziady* was not staged anymore! This was a clear violation of democratic rights, personal freedom, and freedom of speech.

The Warsaw University of Technology and other Poles soon joined the strike.

At the polytechnic, the speeches of various student speakers in the great hall calling for a strike began at morning. We announced a strike, and the printing house was prepared. The main building of the University of Technology was barricaded from the inside with various pieces of furniture. Food and drink supplies had to be organized. I got a permit to leave the University of Technology to bring in my car a few boxes of orangeade from the students' Barn Club. It was already evening when the strike leader, Zieliński, and I traveled in my car to other Warsaw universities. We threw leaflets among students, and Zieliński delivered a speech, stating that the press was lying and that constitutional rights were being violated in so-called Democratic Poland.

When we returned, thousands of people stood in front of the polytechnic, supporting the striking students. There were banners of workers from Żerań and other factories. Then I felt a strange, joyful feeling. I was fully convinced that we were fighting for a just cause. I did not think about the dangers and the consequences.

We joined the strikers with a friend. On the second floor of the main building, baskets were lowered on a string, and people from the street put food, cigarettes, and money into them. Some fastened banners, others burned newspapers, shouting to the public that the press was lying. "Down with communism!" they yelled. Night came, and we went to sleep on bare floors.

The next day began with speeches in the morning. In the big hall, students spoke. Professors spoke as well, calling for an end to the sit-in strike and telling the strikers to go home. This continued until the very evening. I could see in their faces that people were tired. We were all gathered in the great hall, listening, and agreeing or disagreeing with the speakers.

Someone carelessly pushed a large plaster ball that fell from the second floor, landing among the people standing below. I don't think this was a provocation. Fortunately, no one was hit by this ball. It fragmented, scattering to all sides on the floor. The situation became tense. Someone had a seizure, convulsing on the floor as others tried to save him. At night, the university authorities announced that the polytechnic had been surrounded by special militia units. There was a danger of the police force invading the polytechnic, and then bloodshed would be inevitable.

We started looking for weapons in the form of table legs. It wasn't funny then. The university authorities once again announced that buses were waiting outside and that everyone was guaranteed inviolability and safety if they left the building immediately. One-third of the students folded and left the building, but I stayed inside with the others. We knew what we wanted to achieve, but we didn't know how to do it.

Several times, the dean of the university called on microphones to stop the strike. We knew that the point of the matter had been emphasized very strongly and that further resistance was pointless. At four in the morning, all students decided to leave the University of Technology.

The front door opened, the dean walked in, and the students followed. We walked in silence between long lines of special police armed with clubs, pistols, and machine guns. As a sign of protest, everyone looked upon the cobblestones. After passing through the danger zone, people began to go on their various ways. I quickly went to my car and drove home. That night, there were many arrests in the streets. The student accidents that took place all over Poland in 1968 were the seeds of later events in the Gdańsk Shipyard on the way to true democracy.

The next day, as if nothing had happened, I went to the Warsaw University of Technology. There were piles of dilapidated furniture in the hall. There was a large sign on the door stating that the Warsaw University of Technology was closed for two weeks and classes were canceled.

We expected arrests; however, among the students of the Warsaw University of Technology they never came. Authorities had to shut down and kick out many future engineers. Zieliński was arrested and sentenced to two years in prison. Authorities announced in the press that he was insane, which was, of course, nonsense. He was a student at SGPiS. It was also announced that the student riots were a Jewish provocation, and an anti-Zionist attack was started. This was also not true, as I and many other Poles were fighting for just cause.

With such views and bravado in life, I knew that sooner or later I would go to prison. But at that time, I hadn't thought of going to America yet.

During the summer holidays, I worked in Mielno in Koszalin as a lifeguard. There were always a lot of friendly girls around our rescue station. The profession of a rescuer had something exotic and of great adventure about it, and there were always admirers around the rescuers.

As it was said then, Mielno was ruled by rescuers. They were one for all and all for one when there were fights, which were quite frequent. I was walking down the street when a pretty girl with a guy was walking in front of me. I said something nice to her, and her companion growled something at me. I stopped and asked if he wanted something. He must have offended me, because I hit him so hard that he knocked over a fence. As if nothing had happened, I continued on my way.

The next day, the news spread that one of the rescuers had beaten a policeman, and a uniformed officer went to identify him. We woke up at eight in the morning and stood in a row as the policeman walked by and looked everyone in the face. Finally, he stood in front of me and said, "This is the bald one," because I shaved my curly hair during the summer vacation. It was not difficult for him to recognize me. I spent half a day at the militia station. When in this policeman's room, I said that without a uniform it does not look like this. As an apology, I invited him to dinner. After a while, he agreed, and we agreed to meet at the Meduza dancing café.

We got new plastic rescue boats. There were eight of them on the beach, smelling fresh, yet to be tried. There was a black flag up, indicating a gale and big waves, and no one was on the beach. On such days, rescuers were most often bored. Someone had the idea to try out the new lifeboats. One by one, they tried to go out, and at first, the white waves capsized the light boats.

I bet my friend a case of beer that I could go farther into the sea. There was a cold wind, and wearing a tracksuit top, I started to row quickly from the shore. A high, strong wave was placing the boats sideways, and then the next one was capsizing them. The technique to avoid this was to keep the boat perpendicular to the waves at all times. I rowed only with my right arm, so fast and hard that I could meet the next wave at perpendicular. I managed this for quite a long time and ended up two hundred meters from shore, on the high seas. I decided to go back to the shore, but the current was implacable. It was a struggle between a small man and nature.

I was on the way to the shore, and I had another fifty meters to go when my arm started to become painful and lost efficiency. The raging sea turned the boat over, and I found myself several meters away. I swam well and didn't lose my head. I gathered the oars and put them under the boat and climbed onto the bottom of the boat myself. I was lucky that the current took me right toward the shore. Under such conditions, it was impossible to steer the boat. I approached the rocky coastal breakwaters, and thirty meters in front of the rocks, I jumped off the bottom of the boat and swam to the shore on my own. The boat broke on the rocks, and we told the manager that we had been doing stormy trials of the new equipment.

When I was working on the beach in Bulgaria as a lifeguard,

I noticed a very interesting phenomenon. During a hot day and very high waves, the red flag was in force, and it was forbidden to enter the water. My job was outside a luxury hotel, where only Germans lived. I saw that these people could not withstand the heat of the sun and began to enter the water.

The lifeguard on the beach has almost absolute power. However, I compromised and allowed them to go only knee deep in the water to cool off. They were content to enter the water at all. They thanked me, and I had no problem with them anymore because no one was more than knee deep in the water.

The next day, under the same weather conditions, they transferred me to another position, where the Russians were themselves. They also went into the water, so I used the same tactic of letting them enter the water only up to their knees. I saw two or three swimming in deep water, and I threw them out of the water, but the situation repeated itself. I had a hard day dealing with them. This is how I concluded that these two nations have different disciplines.

During similar storm conditions, I saved the life of an Italian girl who was drowning in the vicinity of the shore after being hit by a huge wave. When I pulled her out, she was half awake, but I noticed that she was a pretty girl; she was definitely worth the sacrifice.

About twenty of us paramedics met at 7:30 a.m., ready for work. As part of the warm-up, we were all supposed to swim to the one-hundred-meter buoy and back. Later, everyone went to their workplaces. We had a silent deal with my Bulgarian partner.

In the morning there were no people on the beach yet, so only one per station was enough. The other one at that time slept a little under the umbrella, and then later we changed. Most often, we spent our evenings at nightclubs or discos, remaining there until late into the night.

During my studies, I went for the first time beyond the Iron

Curtain, where, although it sounds strange, at the age of twenty or so I found out what life outside the Polish People's Republic looked like—in short, normal life.

It all started when I was earning money as a lifeguard during the summer holidays, first in Mielno, and then in Sunny Beach in Bulgaria, where I met a German from West Berlin. His name was Kurt, and he was a refugee from East Germany living in West Berlin. At first I thought he was gay, as he asked for my trunks for swimming, but it turned out that this guy just liked me so much that he decided to send me an invitation. In this way, I was able to go to Norway the following year. I know it seems complicated why a German from West Berlin might invite someone to Norway, but those were the times. West Berlin was in disgrace because of the Communist authorities, and I would probably not get a passport upon receiving an invitation from there. My main goal was to go beyond the so-called *demoludy*, so Norway was as good as any other country.

In the beginning, I stayed with Kurt's friend's parents, who provided me with food. It seemed that they did not expect anything in return, so it was only out of goodwill and boredom that I helped them a bit around the house.

I built a wall of stones, trimmed the hedge, and collected roses for wine. My hands were badly pierced during the rose collection. I'm not sure food every day and a glass of the wine fully compensated for this injury.

Shortly after I arrived in Norway, Kurt made a phone call from Berlin. He informed me that everything was already prepared for me—that is, a job and a flat—to come to Germany. I was surprised by this turn of events because we had never talked to him about leaving permanently. It was all about an interesting vacation, after which I intended to return to Politecnic, especially since I had only a year to finish. Kurt called several more times, renewing the offer, and finally he was offended for good.

My hosts were on vacation at the time, and I was taking care of their house and their rattler dog. When they returned from Germany, they unexpectedly asked me to cover all the costs of my stay. This was related to my refusal to go to Germany, and of course I paid.

I moved to Dramen, a beautiful mountain town forty kilometers from Oslo. I got a job at a nearby transformer factory that paid $1.50 an hour. The Norwegians were kind to me, and I satisfied my urge to earn hard currency. I remember I even managed to impress the manager when I upgraded his winding measuring instrument.

I spent the weekends hiking in the mountains or at parties with my Norwegian friends. There I was meeting with a young Norwegian woman, a local teacher, who had intentions of marriage toward me.

While I was earning money from rotten capitalism, traveling, and having romances, socialism was killing people. It was December 1970 when I initially thought that what the Norwegian press was writing was propaganda. I couldn't believe the military could fire at a crowd getting off an electric train!

My stay in Norway lasted a bit longer, and it was enough for me to be summoned to Mostowski Palace upon my return. In a darkened room, an agent wearing glasses confused me with the mud. "You stayed abroad illegally! We'll put you in the file for fugitives." Well, I swallowed that bitter pill. I assumed trips abroad would probably be out of the question for some years. Today I realize that my conversation at the Pałac Mostówski was a similar curiosity to the lard being confiscated from the old lady's neighbor.

Fortunately, I was able to pass my outstanding exams, so my Norwegian trip did not require me to repeat the year. I returned to my usual student life and student entertainment, part of which was my favorite skiing trip to Zakopane. It was there that I met a seventeen-year-old blonde named Marysia. She was pretty and artistically gifted; she won an ice sculpting competition. She is the mother of my eldest son, Marcin Rafał, who today lives with me in the States.

A year after my stay in Norway, I went to Vilnius for a change, where I encountered the Soviet reality. I experienced my first shock on a Soviet train. Namely, I was sitting politely in an empty compartment. A handbag with sandwiches in it was lying next to me until suddenly a menacing conductor entered and roared at me, "You sit by the window and the bag is on the top shelf!" I naively asked if they had such rules here, but the only answer I heard was "*Nu* come on!"

Then, in Vilnius, I entered a store where one could buy items for currency. "You *otkuda* drove?" the clerk asked distrustfully. I explained that I was from Poland, which as it turned out was tantamount to confessing to a crime. "You have no right to enter," said the seller, "You should not have any dollars!"

On the list of rights, I was also deprived a trip to Leningrad. I wanted to go there to visit the Hermitage Museum, but a police-man instructed me that since I had received the invitation from Vilnius, I should stay in Wilno and not wander anywhere. If I tried to go to Leningrad, I would go to jail!

Fortunately, I met a nice conductor who smuggled me in some-how in her service compartment, and thanks to that I visited the famous museum. The conductor expected, I suspect, some sort of compensation, but unfortunately, for my taste, she was too fat.

I defended my master's thesis on March 13, 1973, a Friday. I am not superstitious, and I tried not to notice this date. I received a red-leather-bound original diploma stating that I had earned a master of science degree in electrical engineering.

With this diploma, I started working at Fabryka Samochodow Osobowych in Żerań, first as an apprentice in a design and con-struction office with a monthly salary of two thousand zlote, and then as a normal engineer; my salary then jumped to two hundred more.

My first project was electric barriers which were intended to be installed in all of the factory gates. I worked in a hectic rush so that the first barrier could function at the main gate before July 22, which was the day the Communists had their great holiday.

It had been only a few days since I received the project when a certain Dysza, director of the Electrical Department, called me. "You are the one designing the barriers?"

I eagerly confirmed this, feeling honored by recognition from such an important person.

"So have you finished the project?"

This was pure nonsense; How could it be finished if I had just received it? I told the headmaster the obvious, and then a storm of anger broke out. From the load of curses he threw at me, I remember one for its color and almost baroque poetics: "If I chase you, water in your ass will boil!" said Mr.—sorry, Comrade—Dysza. It stunned me because I never thought that engineers could talk to each other using that kind of language.

After five months of work, I was offered a career promotion. I became a master in the battery room and Internal Transport Department. Under my leadership, there were fifty workers and three hundred electric carts supplying the assembly line with the necessary parts. The responsibility was enormous, the working conditions were unhealthy and dangerous, and there was no money. The 4,500 zlote I earned was the equivalent of forty dollars! Unfortunately, in the People's Republic of Poland, that was a normal salary for an engineer.

People working on battery carts were at risk of lead poisoning, which is why my workers received cash allowances and a daily ration of soup. As a mental laborer, I was deprived of these benefits, even though I inhaled the lead fumes equally with them.

I once met my immediate supervisor on a tram. "You know

what, buddy Welcel?" he said to me. "You have a good chance of being promoted to the head of the department."

However, his further words made it clear that for me to be promoted, I had to join the party. Well, it was no news for me, because I had already received a party application in the design office. Everyone took them. I simply could not go against my beliefs. "I would rather not," I answered the boss evasively. "After all, I am a believer, and I go to church."

"But, my friend Welcel, that is no obstacle," he explained, undaunted. At that time, the Polish United Workers' Party, out of an effort to increase the number of members, did not adhere so strictly to the requirement of atheism.

I have been wondering for a long time about the sense, or rather the nonsense, of the functioning of the factory and the economy in general being about the filling of managerial positions party card decides.

Walking around the FSO premises, I saw enormous amounts of waste. Brand-new Fiat parts rusted in the open air or were stolen en masse. Workers drank during working hours or slept off their hangovers without fear of being laid off. In the People's Republic of Poland, the right to work was constitutionally guaranteed, so no one respected work. It was also not respected by the managers, who were more interested in party careers than in economic results.

It was getting close to vacation, so I started planning a trip around Europe. I bought a new Fiat from the factory, composed thanks to my connections in the rally world and a bribe of the best parts provided for the so-called export version. I supervised the construction of my car, which allowed me to save the tuned engine intended for me, as the workers had already put it into another car body. I gave the brigade for a drink for supper, and a miracle happened. They put it back where it belonged. The operation took them about five minutes, and each minute of belt downtime cost the factory a million. I'm curious whether the numbers would have been be similar at a Detroit factory.

At the same time, I was dealing with travel formalities, and there were a lot of them.

I was going to find survivors for alimony, which I paid for Marcin, and for the amount due for my studies. Universities in the Polish People's Republic were free of charge, but after graduating, one had to work in one's learned profession for three years. Those who did not make up for these three years but wanted to go abroad should have paid a deposit or just introduced a giraffe. The authorities were well aware of the fact that there was a high risk that graduates from the West would not come back. Later, already under martial law, the obligation to reimburse the state for the costs of education was also imposed on people who decided to open a business instead of working for pennies in their professions.

After dealing with the formalities, I held a banquet for my friends. Thanks to two friends who were daughters of the deputy prime minister, it was held in the governmental holiday center in Jadwisin. We sipped cognac and bathed in a nice, large swimming pool, and our safety was supervised by soldiers from the so-called Vistula Unit.

This is how, in a place reserved for the owners of the People's Republic of Poland, I said good-bye to the People's Republic of Poland forever.

CHAPTER 2

EUROPEAN TRAVELS

★ ★ ★

I had not yet made up my mind to leave Poland permanently. I was just planning a month of vacation in Western Europe. I and my ex-girlfriend and future wife (complicated, right?) ventured into capitalism. We had six hundred dollars and a full trunk of canned goods.

Before crossing the border, we stopped at the Hotel Mercure in Poznań. Although I had not planned my escape to the West yet, some intuition told me that this was probably my last night in Poland. Similarly, when I was eating tripe in a roadside restaurant in the morning, I thought it was my last Polish meal.

Inside me, it seemed as if two personalities were fighting with each other. One said, "Leave, do not come back; it will be there somehow!" The second appealed, "Think about it, don't risk it; it is your homeland!"

In East Berlin, under the influence of emotion and staring, I ran against the flow of traffic on the highway. It was early in the morning, there were hardly any cars on the freeway, and I corrected my mistake in time by backing off quickly. However, when I left the ramp, a German policeman stopped me and demanded I pay the fine. I insisted that I did not understand a word of German and that I did not have any marks. After a while, he waved his hand impatiently and told me to drive away.

In Berlin, I ate a pork chop with pineapple for the first time in my life. I even liked it. I figured that the first step to becoming a worldly man was to let go of culinary prejudices.

We had West German visas, but we were not allowed into West Berlin. The border guard demanded a special pass. So we decided to take some photos in front of the Brandenburg Gate. A hundred meters in front of the wall separating Berlin, there was a metal railing; I asked my girlfriend, Ewa, to sit on it, and I aimed my lens at her. However, I did not have time to snap the photo before a Soviet soldier with a machine gun came between us. He ordered Ewa to descend from the railing and growled that photography was not allowed here.

Twelve years later, I found myself under that wall again, only on the other side of it. Nobody guarded or forbade anything there, and the wall was dotted with anticommunist inscriptions. I remember that in the quiet of the park, I allowed myself to pee on this symbol of the Iron Curtain. I laugh now when I say that this was probably the reason it soon fell into ruins.

What I saw on the border between East Germany and West Germany reminded me of a concentration camp. There were several rows of barbed wire in a strip of about two kilometers. The East German guards told us to get out of the car. They searched the trunk thoroughly and checked the underside of the chassis with mirrors. They asked what we were carrying, and they were quite rude.

Finally we crossed the border, and suddenly I was so relieved. A few years later, I realized that it was then that unknown powers lifted the overwhelming boulder of the past from me. From that moment on, even unconsciously, I began to feel and think like a free man. I even said aloud to myself, "Now you can kiss me!"

It was a beautiful time. We visited Germany, Belgium, the Netherlands, Switzerland, France, and Italy with Ewa. We took a lot of photos. For three months, we wandered around Europe, living on four hundred dollars. Only when you are young and courageous can you travel like this. We slept in sleeping bags on fold-out car seats and used our water supplies for daily washing. Once a week, we would go to the hotel to take a good bath and rest, and we would then continue our wandering.

We wanted to see everything: museums, monuments, famous battlefields. Each local map included a list of points of interest; these were our guides.

When the government released Poles to the West, it was as if they were being released from their cage. There were so many problems related to the trip that it turned into a life event.

We had a nice adventure in Hanover. After a few hours walking around the city, we returned to the car and, exhausted, we dozed off in the seats. Suddenly, a middle-aged man knocked on the glass and said something in German.

We understood the word "*kawa*," meaning that he wanted to invite us for a coffee. We went to his house on the plot, and for almost an hour we struggled to keep the conversation going with the help of our poor German. Suddenly, our host turned to his dog and spoke in Polish. It turned out that he used to live in Łódź, and from that moment on, the conversation went smoothly. He suggested that we spend the night in his cabin, to which we gladly agreed. In return, I gave him a bottle of Polish vodka. He was pleased with the gift, and we said good-bye very warmly.

In Germany, I experienced for the first time what it means to be stuck in a traffic jam on a motorway. It was the rush hour, when people were leaving work en masse, and suddenly the traffic stopped. We sat in the car as if trapped in a metal box, and for half an hour we didn't move even a meter. Finally, I pulled over to the side of the road after deciding to let the others get tired. We decided we would get some food. We did so, and after two hours the traffic on the freeway started to flow normally.

I communicated mostly in English. In Germany and the Netherlands, this was possible, though Belgians and French seemed rather reluctant when hearing this language. In France, a great experience was visiting the Louvre, walking along the Champs Élyseés, having coffee in a roadside café, having a sophisticated dinner in a restaurant, and playing a game in a casino.

There was also a trip to the top of the Eiffel Tower and admiring the Parisian panorama. We spent the night romantically, sleeping in the car in the park under the Eiffel Tower. We also visited the famous Battlefield of Waterloo. Yes, I am aware that I will tell you this a little incoherently, but those days were completely like a kaleidoscope, and it is difficult for me to organize all the impressions that follow one another quickly. From France to Italy, we traveled through the mountains, including a long underground tunnel under Mont Blanc. It was snowing in the Alps and the valley of Italy. On the same day, we were greeted by the sun and the green of the vineyards.

Italy is a country of lively, cheerful, and kind people. In terms of character, they were a bit like Poles. It's just that we didn't pick on girls so pushily and we don't lose our heads when we saw pretty blondes. The Italians, when they saw a the fair-haired lady, would call to her, whistle to stop her car in the middle of the road, and run after her.

Ewa is blonde, so we did not have to wait long for such antics in Rome. I left her alone for a moment, and a handsome Italian guy spotted her. When I appeared, he showed no aggression. On the contrary, he politely introduced himself to me. Then the four of us traveled with him and his girlfriend on weekends to Ostria on the Adriatic; his uncle had a villa there that at that time was empty.

Our new friend's name was Mauro, and he was a typical

southern boy by character and outlook. I remember being stuck in a traffic jam on the way to Ostria. Mauro did not think for a long time; he jumped out of the car, waving his arms, stopped the movement from the opposite direction, and indicated for me to drive across.

For a moment, I wondered whether he had a mental issue, but in this situation, it was an effective solution. Another time, Mauro leaned out of the car, shouting to a passing driver, "Gumma! Gumma!" The other driver, thinking that he had a flat tire, pulled over to the side of the road, and our companion was enjoying the trick like a child. This Italian was crazy and funny!

My internal struggle to choose whether or not to return to Poland was resolved by an unexpected accident. While we visited the Colosseum, our car was robbed. We lost all our money and all our documents except for our passports. Losing my engineering diploma hurt me the most, so I searched for it for a long time among the historic ruins, in vain. In the ruins, I found only a prostitute's den and a line of waiting soldiers. "City of ruins, whores, and thieves!" I said angrily about Rome.

I reported the theft to the Italian police and the Polish Embassy. I asked the consul for a gas loan so that I could return to my country. It turned out that this kind of help was not provided, and the consul advised me to ask my Italian friends for money. Then I made my decision and directed my next steps to the US Embassy!

The American consul refused to issue me a visa. He argued that I had not returned to work in Poland on time so I probably intended to stay in the USA permanently. He sent me one floor up, to the Emigration Department. At this point, I no longer had a choice. The threads linking me to Poland finally broke, and I started to deal with emigration formalities.

We were helped by a Christian organization that paid for our accommodation. We moved in with two Russian Jews. Like

many fellow believers, they had emigrated from the Soviet Union
to Israel, but in Italy, they had changed their minds and suddenly
wanted to go to America. Wealthy American Jews helped them
financially.

At first we had separate apartments and only visited each
other. Misza, short and stocky, played guitar and sang Russian
songs. He said that he was part of a militia and that he had been
sentenced to fifteen years in a labor camp for a fight with a knife.
Wańka was his opposite—a big, fat man with the soul of an artist.
He made bas reliefs with copper sheeting. All in all, they were both
nice companions, and we felt good in their company.

Once, Misha and Wanka went for Roman street prostitutes.
Misha, a smart man, paid two thousand lire, took the whore to the
gate, and did his job. Wańka, on the other hand, had more culture.
He politely asked, "Quanto costa, seniora?"

The whore, to whom no one spoke with equal attention, took it
as a mockery and chased poor Wanka away. "No one has insulted
her since the senior," laughed Miszka.

The owner of the house we stayed in was tight-fisted. For example, she demanded an additional fee for a bath. Once I harshly
told her what I thought about this and broke up between us.

"Don't worry," said Miszka when he heard about this. "In a
few years, you will come here from America, spit on a ten-dollar
bill, and stick it on her forehead."

Later, the organization supporting us stopped paying for the
apartment and suggested that we move to the camp in Trieste.
As we wanted to stay in Rome for some more time, we moved
to Miszka, Wańka. Initially it was idyllic, but later Misha began
to approach Ewa. I decided that there was no point in risking
conflict, and we moved to Trieste. On the way, we quickly visited
Venice in the American way. It cost us forty dollars, as he was
carrying a parking ticket. Venice lives off tourists.

There was a transit camp in Trieste, where they waited for a visa to the chosen destination country. Camps of this kind were sponsored by Western countries, mainly America. One could get room and board there.

The conditions in the camp were quite primitive, but no one protested, knowing that the situation was temporary though it would last for some time. One could meet all kinds of people there, from the intelligentsia to the complete rabble. There was, for example, an engineer who escaped with his family by driving full-throttle through the border checkpoint between Yugoslavia and Italy. There were people who for many days crossed the "green border," wandering in the forests and brush. There was a policeman, and a criminal who spent a year in prison for his previous attempt to escape from the People's Republic of Poland. Interestingly, he was the first of the entire Polish group to receive political asylum in Italy.

The emigre authorities conducted long interrogations aimed at catching possible Communist spies. Medical examinations were also carried out, mainly for infectious diseases. It all went on and on, so the boredom was terrible. In order not to fall into apathy, I read a lot. In addition, I signed up for an English language course. It was better than spending time talking to fellow countrymen, because they often made me pessimistic. To this day, like a bad dream, I remember a guy who constantly tried to convince me that in America I would have to scrub the toilets.

We stayed in Trieste for about a month; then, after completing the initial formalities, we moved to another camp in Latina. We had known for some time that Ewa was pregnant. This brought us closer to each other and strengthened our mutual feeling. We knew that we would not part, and together it was easier to go through the hardships of a foreign country.

There were no such rigors in Latina as there had been in Trieste. We had a common room with Ewa, and we could go outside the camp for days without any restrictions. I felt like a tourist again and took advantage of the freedom. I visited, among other places, Pisa and the famous Capri.

A fight with a certain bully from Warsaw is an unpleasant memory I have of Latina. As I said, there were different elements in the camps, and if you didn't drink vodka with some of them, they treated you like a freak. Despite the obvious brazen provocation, I tried not to react, because fighting could result in expulsion from the camp and other consequences. However, when during my shift (we all had work shifts; I was responsible for cleaning on a given day) he maliciously spilled the contents of the ashtrays on the floor, my nerves gave up. I told the bastard to get outside the camp wall, and I knocked him out there. As you can see, my boxing training was useful for something. From then on, the camp rabble felt respect for me, and the provocations were never repeated.

The wait for our American visas was extended, and I did not want to allow our child to be born in the camp. Ewa came up with the idea that, as I had been born in Germany, I should apply for the right to stay in Germany. This had its good aspects, because it would be closer to my family, but the German consul refused to deal with me. In West Germany, as he said, the parents' law was in force, not the law of the land, and my parents were Poles. As a consolation, he added that as an American citizen with German birth, they would be happy to accept me later. Now, after nineteen years in the States, I have no intention of using this offer and moving to Germany permanently. Europe, as a place of emigration, has never attracted me. Unlike the USA, there is too much prejudice there in terms of nationality.

We could have settled relatively easily in South Africa, which welcomed white people. As a holder of an engineering degree, I was offered a monthly salary of $700. However, I did not take advantage of it: I was scared by the disproportion between the white and Black populations in South Africa and the thought of a revolution related to it. Years later I could see my fears were right. Today, the future of this wealthy country is suspended in a vacuum.

However, the Christian organization that supported us, was informed that I would go to South Africa. This was a form of pressure to accelerate their efforts on the "American front." At the same time, in Rome, I asked a priest I knew from the Order of Marian Fathers to marry us. Apart from emotional reasons, I also knew that Ewa would not receive an American visa as a single woman, .

I gave the engagement ring to my fiancée in Pompeii, at the foot of the menacing Vesuvius, which had covered this city with lava and ash centuries ago. We were married in the Vatican.

I remember that my engine went out on the very border of the Papal States. Whether it was an omen or just the fuel filter I don't know. I was stubborn, waited a while, and managed to get the car started. Thanks to this, we made it without any problems.

We were married by Father Zenon, a wonderful man and a great friend of immigrants, and two other Polish priests. It was solemn, without any great pomp. After the wedding, the Marian Fathers organized a party for us in the convent. During our wedding night, Ewa and I dreamed that our honeymoon would be a trip to America.

Our dreams came true when our visas arrived. After a six-hour delay due to a strike by Roman airport workers, a mighty Boeing carried us across the Atlantic. Our European chapter was ending. I left behind the times of trials, experiments, and the formation of views. I left Poland physically, but I took her in my heart to a new, unknown motherland.

CHAPTER 3

IN AMERICA

★ ★ ★

We were welcomed in New York by a representative of our Christian organization. Ewa received a green card, but I had to wait three more years for the document. The migration agency made a mistake in including Ewa among people coming to their immediate families. Maybe they thought that I was already in America, and she was coming to me.

In New York, we were to spend the night at a hotel, and in the morning we were to fly to Chicago, where my friend would be waiting for us at the airport. I was surprised by how quickly the girl at the hotel reception desk worked. She answered phone calls, wrote letters, and handed over the keys at such a pace that in Poland it would have been said that "the robot was on fire in her hands." I was even a bit scared at the thought that maybe all of America worked like that.

In our room, we felt hungry. We had only a can of sardines left from the trip. I went bravely to the hotel restaurant to buy some bread. I was convinced that I knew English.

I told the waiter that I wanted to buy a piece of bread, and he mentioned several types for me and asked which one I meant. Honestly, I was completely stupid at this point. "Any kind," I replied eloquently. The waiter finally decided for me, and I got the bread. In America, rye bread is not popular; they mainly eat wheat bread, as soft as cotton wool and not very suited to our Polish tastes.

Another hotel attraction that we genuinely laughed at was the shaky bed. After dropping twenty-five cents in a slot, the bed vibrated for ten minutes. This was supposed to give a feeling of general relaxation, like a massage. Someone might have bad thoughts at this point, but the bed builders just wanted to relax.

The next morning, we departed from Chicago on a modern, clean plane from United. Don't worry; nothing is free in America. I later had to pay our organization back for the costs of our trip in installments for two years.

At O'Hare Airport in Chicago, my friend Magda was waiting with her fiancé Mietek. I still knew Magda from Poland; during our student days, we even dated each other. It was a nice surprise to see her years later.

Though I did not know it at the time, this meeting had been arranged, by our Christian organization. I also did not know that Magda, as an American citizen, had been asked to sponsor us. She agreed and immediately offered me a $100 loan at the airport so that I could survive the beginning. I thanked her because so far I hadn't needed a loan so much. In Italy, I sold my Fiat, and I saved money from some small camp jobs, so I had $2,000.

As we drove through the city, I was surprised that the streets were so wide and that the cars were so large and so many. Mietek took us home in a large Cadillac. It was an old Polish community district, supposedly beautiful in the past, the so-called Polonia Triangle at the junction of Ashland, Division, and Milwaukee. Currently, this district is inhabited by Blacks, Puerto Ricans, and the remnants of the old Polish community. The first two groups do not have good results in America. Magda and Mietek warned me that the street was dangerous even in broad daylight. At that time, I didn't know who the threat was, so I calmly went for a walk. What I saw did not make me feel optimistic.

The neighborhood looked like one huge garbage can: broken windows, burned-out houses, and drunkards and drug addicts lying on street benches. I thought it was even worse than in my native Praga. I currently live in a wealthy district in Southern California, so I have a comparative scale. I can say that I know the length and breadth of America, with its strengths and weaknesses.

We stayed in Mietek's house in a small room measuring three by three meters. It was May, when the heat and the humidity of the air deprives one of one's strength—especially an unadapted European. We sat with Ewa in this cramped room without air conditioning. My brain was boiling, and she, eight months pregnant, was barely hot. Added to this was the unpleasant awareness that I was unemployed and did not know where to start. I realized that I had to get to know as many Poles as possible, because they could be a source of information for me.

I quickly realized that my engineering degree was not useful yet. I started applying for jobs, but because I couldn't do any practice in the US, nobody wanted to talk to me seriously. Still, I didn't complain. After all, I was there bent on difficulties. I knew that one had to learn the language and work hard, and that the results would not come until later.

A Pole I knew divorced his wife, a bar singer. He offered me his apartment—two rooms with a kitchen and furniture—for $700, and the rent was $200 a month. The old stuff wasn't worth that amount, but for lack of other solutions, I agreed. In the United States, thanks to the free market and tax breaks, many private rental houses, or apartment houses, have been built. The situation is that supply now exceeds demand. Our new apartment was on the second floor of a solid building and had air conditioning.

We lived in the very center of the Puerto Rican neighborhood. Puerto Rico is not famous for banditry (although their compatriots in Puerto Rico are quite decent people); that is a general opinion. Puerto Rico is an American colony of its own choice; in 1993, the population approved this state of affairs in a plebiscite because of financial benefits. They did not want to join America as the fifty-first state. Racism and the display of ethnic prejudices are prohibited by law; life, however, is life, and hardly anyone decides to live in a Black or Puerto Rican neighborhood where knives and pistols reign supreme.

Americans are generally not chatty, polite, and well mannered. When you speak with a foreign accent, they ask where you are from. That doesn't mean they have prejudices; quite to the contrary, this is how they want to break the ice and have a conversation with you.

In the USA, a person's position is determined primarily by his financial condition. I noticed that nobody here cares about academic titles, as we do in Poland. You may be an uneducated guy here, but if you are successful in business and earn good money, you are a dude. And vice versa, if you have a doctoral degree but you have nothing to put into the pot, they consider you an embarrassment.

It is interesting that despite this outlook, money is hardly ever talked about. For example, management forbids one bragging about one's earnings. The goal of this is to prevent animosity. It is also tactless to ask about earnings. Anyway, what would the purpose of this be? Americans judge themselves based on where and how they live and what cars they drive. At that time, I did not understand this yet and did not attach any importance to the choice of the district I lived in.

In hot, humid summers, it's hard to sleep without air conditioning. You have the impression that you are lying in boiling water. You are sweating. It is difficult to breathe. With air conditioning, you can also catch a cold easily. I came up with the idea of opening the screened window at night and putting a fan in it. That gave me a little bit of a breeze. At the same time, however, there were noises from the street, and in front of our house was a Puerto Rican church where daily, at almost one o'clock in the morning, there was singing and the playing of drums. At first it bothered me a lot, but later I began to fall asleep due to these sounds.

One Sunday, I decided to see a Puerto Rican prayer service. Their priest, who was standing at the door of the church, looked surprised when he saw me but politely shook my hand. I sat down on a pew, and the Mass began. How different from our services it was, though Puerto Ricans are also Catholics! The priest seemed to be speaking at a rally; now and then he would raise his hand and shout, "Hallelujah! Alleluia!" I noticed that despite the loud singing, some of the Puerto Rican children were sleeping on the floor. I ceased to be surprised when I realized that the service would last many hours. Of course, I did not wait for the conclusion and, having acquired a general idea of their customs, left the church.

Of course, I followed the habits of American Poles with even greater interest and I noticed that the old Polish community speaks a strange language, amusingly mixing Polish with English, or, simply put, "Polishing" English words. For example: "I was sitting in the steppes," "I was talking to the blue one," and "give me a mister cola," meaning "call me." Well, foreign words often repeated become ours. I also met compatriots who had recently come from Poland and were in a strange linguistic suspension; they had not learned English yet, but they had already forgotten Polish. Or maybe they consciously refused to admit their native language. I am reminded of an anecdote about them. A young man, after returning from work in Germany, addressed his mother with these words: " ... handed over to a sztrajholce, because I forgot what matches are called in Polish."

I was sitting on the floor with newspapers spread out around me. I was looking through the columns of job advertisements. I called a lot of places where either they didn't want to understand my English or where the job I wanted had already been taken. Americans don't bother to understand foreigners. If you ask for something in the street and you don't pronounce it correctly, they wave their hand and just walk away. In general, there are hardly any people on the street; everyone drives and hardly anyone walks.

In the shop where I wanted to buy a body brush, I repeated for five minutes, "Brush for body, please," with no success. The problem was that I was pronouncing "body" with an English accent, not as the American "bahdy," so the seller did not understand. In America, it is like that. Things are written one way and pronounced another. It's not easy!

I temporarily gave up my ambition to work as an engineer. First I had to practice my language and brush up on a job in local offices to be able to demonstrate American practice. The billion-dollar question was, How could I get an apprenticeship if no one would hire a guy who hadn't gone through an apprenticeship? It was a vicious circle! I called a Jew who had placed an ad in the paper. He had me work for the minimum wage, which at the time was $2.50 an hour. His company specialized in sanding floors, and experience was required. I lied, saying that I had experience.

After drinking coffee in a bar and having a short conversation, we went to work. The boss took the machine in two hands and bent it to show me how to sand the floors. On the same day, together with one American, working in cycles, we sanded a ten-room flat in ten hours. The work was not complicated, but it was very tiring, so I demanded a raise the next day. The boss easily agreed to three dollars an hour. I was paid in cash, not by check, and I was employed illegally, so I was not burdened with any taxes.

In June, when the summer vacation began, we were commissioned to do a whole school's wenge hallway. I remember it as a bad dream! I recall dust and heat, and I was the only one hunched over that damn machine. The long corridor seemed endless, and I was breathless with the heat and effort. When I returned home after ten or twelve hours of this hard work, I immediately undressed and sat down in the bathtub, which I filled with cold water to cool myself off, and it took a few minutes for me to recover.

"You must pay me four dollars an hour!" I demanded firmly. Unfortunately, the boss refused me just as firmly. Then I announced that from Monday I would stop working for him. I hoped he would think it over, soften, and call me over the weekend, but he didn't call, and so I lost my first American job. Later I learned that each subsequent job always pays better.

Sitting at home was not good for my psyche. It's good that the unemployment did not last long; after just two weeks, I got a job as an electrician fitter with a salary of four dollars per hour. This time I was legally employed, and the company was legally paying tax on me.

I worked on the assembly of high-power rectifiers used for electroplating. In my brigade, I was the only white person; the other three were Indian. They told me that they were engineers and they treated this job as something of a temporary arrangement. I never admitted to having my diploma. I knew there was a rule in America that people were employed according to their qualifications. What is the point of training someone at the expense of the company if that person has better professional prospects and will leave at the first opportunity?

Initially, I took the bus to work, but I was already starting to think about buying a car. I wanted a small and economical car, so I thought in European terms. Americans, without exception, preferred large cars in which there is a lot of room. "Why do they need this room?" I wondered. "After all, it's not a ballroom?" But gasoline was fifty cents a gallon back then, so no one cared how much the car was burning.

I was one of the first to buy a four-cylinder Chevrolet Monza in 1975. It was as if I had predicted the energy crash that followed a few years later. The Monza was an American debut in the field of small cars, and the model, as I realized later, was not particularly successful.

In America, everything is easy to buy without money (i.e., in installments), provided that you have a job (i.e., the ability to pay off) and a so-called loan.

Credit is nothing but a good reputation. If you have taken something in the past and repaid it on time, you have credit. Your reliability is recorded in the memory of computers of specialized agencies, such as TRW. Sellers can check on this in a few minutes. The paradox is that the man who pays for everything in cash does not have credit.

I couldn't afford a car with cash, and I needed a giraffe for my installments. Mietek agreed to guarantee my installment. "Where do you work?" asked the seller. "Out of business," replied Mietek, because at that time his café had burned down. The house had survived, however, and that was enough collateral.

All companies that accept payments in installments must protect themselves. If the client stops paying, specialized agencies are called for help, and they repossess the purchased items. A few gentlemen come at night, without saying anything, take, say, the car, and the bank sells it at an auction. This is a completely legal auction.

My first car in America was $3,500 and I drove it all over the place. I took it into my possession after paying the $1,000 down payment. In the States, being without a car is like being without a hand. Statistically, there is one car for every two citizens. This does not have a positive effect on the ecology or the traffic capacity of the streets.

The factories where I worked were located in the center of the Black district. While driving the new car, I learned to listen to Black music. The style of music was called rap, and it was very rhythmic. I like rhythm; maybe that's why dancing—youthful dancing, where the steps are not learned but dictated by something that is in the genes, has always been my passion. That is why Black people are such great dancers—because rhythm is in their nature. Have you noticed how Black people walk in American movies? Isn't it as if they have music playing in their heads all the time? And it is similar with sport here also; the sense of rhythm and the right balance of the body determine the result of the match. I have these qualities, and that's why I was good at sports. On the other hand, friends point out to me that I walk a bit strangely, as if I am leaving my legs behind me. Well, Black people have their dance gait, and I have my sports gait. Both come from a sense of rhythm.

For a month, I had a Polish driving license, then I passed the American exam. I could take the exam in Polish, but I chose English. In this way, I decided to prove to myself that I already knew a little bit.

There was a certain difficulty because it turned out that someone had to bring me to the exam. I asked an American friend to drive me twenty meters to the starting point of the driving test. It turned out that I, who was about to pass the exam, had to teach him this friend to shift gears. On five consecutive attempts, he stalled the engine, but finally he got it.

My coworkers, the Indians, exalted themselves a lot. None of them would answer my morning "Good morning." In general, this race has a great opinion of itself: almost every Indian, of course in his own words, comes from an aristocratic family. I think they need such exaltation mentally because most Americans think they are sloppy and dirty.

I think our animosity stemmed from cultural differences: different chemistry, different diet. For me, the meals they cooked in the microwave just stunk. No, I didn't find their food disgusting; it was just that the spices they used didn't suit my palate as something new and unknown.

For a long time, there were clashes between my Indians and one of the Black people on the job. One day, away from the brigade, I was drilling holes and suddenly I heard quarrelling. Before I had a chance to look, the commotion had already begun. The Black man did not look like a bully, but he made a healthy contribution to four Indians. The fight lasted five minutes and led to considerable devastation in the workshop. The Black employee did not have time to enjoy the victory, because he was almost immediately fired from work. And I had a little satisfaction that the puffed-up Indians were punished.

The manager offered me a standalone restorer job in Chicago. I was given a car and a set of necessary tools. When electroplating factories reported rectifier failure to us, I was sent as a specialist. I liked this new job because it gave me freedom of movement. I also got to know Chicago and learned new things. I even took a special notebook, in which I wrote down newly learned phrases and words. I also quickly grasped the difference between European and American markings on technical drawings. This was the first step to becoming a draftsman.

With the help of a kind Pole, I wrote a résumé. I then copied it on a photocopier and sent copies to all electrical companies looking for draftsmen. Soon after, I secured my first employment interview. Unfortunately, it was to take place during my working hours. In a secluded place, I had to stop the car and change into a suit from my work clothes. Of course, I didn't get a job on my first attempt.

I was asked about my drawings, which of course I didn't have, because how could I if I hadn't worked as a draftsman in America yet? As I already told you, this obligation to prove yourself is a complete paradox! Finally I found the answer. I made a few drawings, supposedly from my factory, which I signed with my name. They bought it. I had finally gotten around the problem of lack of practice. I became a signboard draftsman who already had American experience!

During my trips to Chicago, I met a Czech mechanical engineer who had been working as a welder for ten years. I asked him why he didn't get a job in the office? As a draftsman, I made five dollars an hour, and as a welder, I could earn nine dollars an hour. Then he added that he had a lot of financial needs: housing installments, furniture installments, and so on.

Today I know that his thinking and acting were wrong. After a dozen or so years, I was earning thirty dollars an hour, and he, as a welder, was still making nine dollars an hour. Many people make this mistake; engineers and other specialists, in the pursuit of current earnings, work in areas below their qualifications. Charmed by the wealth of the market and the possibility of buying in installments, they constantly buy things and, of course, constantly have to pay for them. Rushed and busy, they have no time to learn a language or improve their profession. They find themselves on a treadmill, which it becomes more and more difficult to break free from with time. Yes, money is important in America, but it is not the most important thing, and this must not be forgotten. If someone does his job without inner satisfaction just because he is paid, sooner or later he will become apathetic and become disgusted with the job.

It is easier for immigrants to work in engineering in America than in other professions. They do not have their relationships and are sort of independent contractors. Each of us tries to sell ourselves as expensive as possible. Of course, if you ask too much, you might not get a job. American engineers earn between $30,000 and $100,000 a year. Employers are not required to recognize diplomas, as is the case with doctors. Nobody ever asked me for my diploma. What mattered was the résumé and the interview. The best thing to do was to ask for a green card or a US passport as documents authorizing one to work in America. Naturally, an engineer at the company must demonstrate competency; otherwise, he will be dismissed quickly.

The medical profession is the highest-paid profession in the United States. A ten-minute visit costs an average of $100, and statistically, a doctor earns over $200,000 a year. Its interests are guarded by the powerful medical unions and the American Medical Association.

I have always been shocked that I have to spend an entire day's wages for a short visit to the doctor's office. But that's the way it is, and that's why it's better not to get sick in the United States. Of course, there is also free treatment in the so-called district hospitals, which are used by the poorest and only in justified cases.

In the United States, several procedures are performed without much necessity, to benefit doctors. This is the case, for example, in childbirth, where a Cesarean section is almost always performed. The worst part is that the American doctor rarely wants to talk to the patient; he will not even tell you what your temperature is, because why would you need to know.

With my next attempt, I finally got a job as a draftsman. I was earning $5 an hour, and the company had to pay off the middleman, an agency that charged $1,000 for finding me. The truth is, I was looking for the long and painstakingly. I signed a document stating that I would not quit before the end of the year—that is, until I had worked enough to cover the $1,000.

In the company, I drafted control systems. I was learning symbols and familiarizing myself with typical solutions. The pace of work was quite fast. In one day, the entire sheet had to be drafted. I drew with a graphite pencil, called a film pencil, or simply a film, on a thick tracing paper. This was a completely different technique than the one I had learned in Poland. There we used ink on bristol board, which was tedious and time-consuming. Besides that, it was almost impossible to make corrections. In contrast, the film pencil rubbed against the Mylar perfectly.

Copies were made with a high-speed machine. Everything

was designed to reduce the draftsman's effort as much as possible and shorten the working time.

During the nineteen years of my engineering practice, I have watched the constant improvement of office technology. Today we draw with the help of computers, using AutoCAD, and the blue and black lines can be copied using any type of paper. Engineering information is sent over huge distances in seconds thanks to fax, email, and telephone lines, and calculations, tables, and reports are made at the computer. Only one thing has not changed: the use of gray cells by the engineer.

After a year, drawing began to wear me out. It was too templated and mechanical. In addition, there were conflicts with the Ukrainian manager, who came to America as a Pole and was passionate about Polish jokes—jokes showing Poles as the slow, dirty, drunk, and stupid.

"Do you know what a Polish shower is?" He asked me, and after a moment he explained with a chuckle that the punchline related to urination. I said the joke was stupid. A few days later, he fired, me saying I was too slow. I found this strange; I had been fast and accurate for a year, and now suddenly I was slow? Undoubtedly this was the manager's revenge."

This was the only office where I heard polish jokes. If I had worked in factories and dealt with workers, I would probably have heard them more and more often. Less-educated people are eager to make fun of those from different nations, other than the intelligentsia. In America, they laughed one by one at the Jews and the Irish, and now it was the Poles. This is because many people with low culture come to America from various countries.

Communism, poverty, and the backwardness of the PRL did their job. However, I strongly believe that the time will come when the words "Poland" and "Pole" will gain respect in the world. For this, however, we need to improve our economic condition, because this is mainly what allows people to walk with their heads held high. So, to be respected, we must want respect ourselves! We are seeing the fruit of this now in 2022 since Poland has become free of Russian influence and Poland now has the twenty-second largest gross domestic product in the word.

I have been telling those who tell Polish jokes the following joke in return: Do you know why Poles are buried facedown in the ground? So that you can kiss their asses for telling Polish jokes!

Anyway, I am George Welcel, and I am proud of my Polish origin! I will never do as my colleague Wojtek Wrona, who renamed himself Jim Stone in the States. Name changes can be made automatically upon obtaining US citizenship, and Wojtek took this opportunity. He argued that the American name was better suited for business because Poles do not trust Poles. Well, I've lived in the States for almost twenty years, my name is Welcel, and yet people trust me somehow.

With this Mr. Wrona, a.k.a. Stone, I started going to the shooting range, and I even bought myself a .22 caliber High Standard pistol with a scope. Today we have as many as four pistols, and yet I believe that the government should somehow restrict access to firearms, which are too widespread in America.

The statistics of homicides committed with pistols are intimidating, but the free purchase and possession of weapons is guarded by hunting rifle corporations and a constitutional record from more than two hundred years ago, according to which privately held weapons protect citizens from government oppression.

Stone was married to a Polish woman. American girls somehow smelled better to him. I lived for a while in the same building as Stone, in a white working-class neighborhood. Every Sunday, he called me to go with him in his Pontiac Trans-Am to get milk. He had noticed that at a store five miles away, milk was ten cents cheaper per gallon. He did not seem to take into account the cost of fuel in this calculation.

Ewa asked me to go with her to her first gynecological visit in America, to an old Polish doctor. When I started asking him questions about the upcoming delivery, he said he didn't have time to talk to me. Immediately this doctor–patient system stank to me somehow. The doctor did not have time to talk because the clock was ticking away the dollars. He gave me a business card so that I could call when I was going to the hospital with Ewa.

It happened shortly thereafter, at two in the morning. Semiconscious, I jumped out of bed, quickly dressed, called the doctor, and was soon in the car. I was driving very fast, but luckily the streets were empty at this time. In the hospital registration area, a long series of questions about the insurance policy and the form of payment began. I was not allowed in there. I wanted to wait in the corridor but was told to go home. "Everything is okay," I was told. "We'll call you when it's over." And indeed, in the morning, when I was assembling the crib, the doctor called to tell me that a son had been born to me. I brought them home from the hospital, and as a happy father, I took care of washing, cooking, and cleaning, as well as feeding and bathing the baby. Ewa could not do all of this because she was still very weak after giving birth. Later, when she gained strength, she also preferred not to help me, and I had my own paid job. Against this background, the first misunderstandings and quarrels began between us. The most important thing was that the toddler was growing healthily. To celebrate our stay in America, I named him Roger Dominik.

At the same time, I started to maintain closer contact with the Polish. I was an active founder of a group affiliated with the Polish National Alliance. I used to come to the meetings with Ewa and baby Roger in a stroller. The president of the Polish American Congress, Mr. Mazewski appeared at the ceremonial establishment of the new group, but our little one was the pride of the ceremony.

Many friends were attracted to the first general meeting. We had to establish a name for the group and set up various formal details. As usually happens in our Polish environment, there were disputes and quarrels over minor details. It was discussed at length whether the group should be called Generation or Generation-68.

Out of the entire group of thirty, I was the only one who had participated in the student strikes of 1968, and I felt that this date was not worth the argument that arose during the vote. Eventually, the name Generation was adopted, and immediately afterward someone expressed the view that the "red rags" came from Poland. Some of the people, indignant, left the room, and a split arose, as a result of which two groups were formed. One was more concerned with politics, and the other, called by me the Entertainment group, focused on organizing social life. I belonged to both of them. With the Generation group, we organized picnics and ski trips, but also protest marches in front of the PRL consulate. We marched in front of the consulate building carrying a black coffin before other groups vandalized the consulate with red paint.

Regardless of practicing this type of activity, I could not forget that I was on the pavement again (i.e., out of work). I could not count on anyone's help, because in the profession of an engineer, protection does not work very well.

At a party, I met an American, and during a social conversation, I realized that he was vice president of an agency employing technical staff. It was a turning point in my life. When I said that I was an unemployed electrical engineer, this new friend handed me a business card and asked me to call Monday.

Thanks to this unexpected help, I got a job as a design engineer in downtown Chicago at Kaiser Engineering. I took the underground train there. The underground railway, the so-called subway, is the site of many criminal excesses, especially at night. Fortunately, nothing happened to me during these years, probably because I was not a pretty girl.

I liked the job. Design skills were required of me. To cope with the task, I had to constantly learn. Contract work was temporary, and usually it was about carrying out one specific project; I would earn a few dollars more per hour, and the work would have more requirements.

I did not have to be afraid of these increased requirements; after all, I was a professional. I was earning $8.50 an hour—a clear improvement over the draftsman's salary.

All the time, I was wondering about additional income. And once, on the street, I heard a fragment of a conversation between two Poles:

"I bought a house, fixed it up a bit, and sold it."

"How much did you earn on it?"

"twenty thousand dollars."

Sometimes it's worth listening to what people are talking about. I began to wonder if I, too, could make such a deal. I had all my assets set aside—$4,000—and I was told by a real estate agency that the cheapest home in a relatively decent neighborhood would cost around $32,000 and the down payment would be at least a quarter of the value. I remembered that my friend Kazik, an engineer, had 5 percent of his money in the bank. I offered him an interest rate of 7 percent. "You lend me four thousand dollars for a year, and I will pay you back at a rate higher than the bank's." He agreed without hesitation, and the whole deal was done in the old-fashioned way of word of honor and a handshake. Kazik knew that the newly bought house would be the pledge.

Even my late grandfather Ignacy taught me that in business you always have to keep your word. Honest trades can be repeated many times, but cheating can be done only once before you are already offside. It is a pity that this rule is sometimes forgotten by young Polish businessmen.

Buying a house was a very important decision in my life, but it turned out to be right. We sat for quite a long time in the real estate office, browsing through a thick book of offers. I identified three houses in a white neighborhood at an affordable price. It was a winter evening, and a snowstorm was taking place. Regardless of that, we went to see them immediately. We liked the third one the most; it was brick and had two offices downstairs and a six-room apartment upstairs, and it cost only $35,000. An elderly couple of Norwegian origin lived there. Within ten minutes, I decided to offer them $32,500 and $500 in cash. Later that evening, the agent called us to say that the offer had been accepted. It was all so easy that I had a strange feeling that it was too easy.

I had bought my first house after a year and a half in the States! This amazed the entire Polish community. People lived here for years, renting apartments, enriching the American owners. You could say that I set an example for the Polish community. After I did so, more and more compatriots started to buy houses.

It was one of the better investments back then. The houses were still relatively inexpensive, and their prices rose with each passing year. I thought logically that I had to live somewhere, so why not at home? And if you are buying a house, why not consider it a business? Buy cheap in a nice neighborhood, renovate a bit, wait for the prices to rise, and sell at a profit.

Over time, I even educated myself in this direction and obtained the highest real estate broker licenses for the state. I helped my friends and made the investments myself. In total, so far I have flipped six houses in the United States, earning several hundred thousand dollars on these transactions.

There is a category of people who spend all their money immediately on consumption, buying furniture, clothes, cars, and the like. I assumed that it was better to invest.

In America, there is a saying about guns and butter. A gun is an investment, and butter is a symbol of pleasures. If you invest well—that is, shoot well—you can then have as much butter as your heart desires. Think about it for a moment!

Unfortunately, right after I moved, I understood why the price of the house was so low. There was a crack in the wall between the main part of the building and the brick extension of porch. One could fit a fist into it. Experts I consulted decided that the reason for the crack was the weakness of the steel columns supporting the extension, which had allowed the extension to settle into the ground. In their opinion, the renovation would cost me thousands.

Well, I went the more economical way and hired a cheap Polish handyman to fix the doors, floors, and that fatal crack. In addition, I rolled up my sleeves myself and went to work on the electric, plumbing, and painting. I spent almost all my weekends on the ladder, but I didn't complain, as it was my first home and so worth the sacrifice. In the end, with hard work, I got it right in six months. And then my mother-in-law showed up.

I was standing on the ladder, filling the last holes in the wall, when Ewa brought her from the airport. She said hello and walked around the whole apartment.

"But you bought a shack," she said. I had to grab the ladder to keep my balance.

"I see that Mother does not know the American market," I said, in my mind thinking, *Well, my mother-in-law came to visit.*

Before the war, Ewa's mother was the owner of a tenement house in Warsaw. After 1945, the Communists nationalized most of the private estates, including her house and my grandfather's house in Legionowo. It was not exactly nationalization so much as the inclusion of the so-called extraordinary lease procedure. The owner was still the owner, while the house was inhabited by tenants who paid symbolic rents that in no way matched the real costs of operating the premises. As a result, such houses, of course, fell into disrepair. In 1990, I saw what was left of my grandfather's house in Legionowo, which had once been the pride of the neighborhood. It was more or less as devastated as the rest of Poland during forty-five years of Communist rule.

But let's go back to America, where construction and housing were governed by healthy market laws. As I mentioned, my new house had two offices downstairs. I rented one to a gynecologist, and the other—which was less attractive, as it was accessed from the backyard—I adapted into an apartment.

One day, some drunkards from a nearby bar broke a window in the office. The doctor demanded that I put in a new one. I did not want to pay a glazier and decided to do it myself.

After work, I climbed a ladder to take measurements. And then, right by the palm of my hand, I saw a naked woman—my doctor's patient. I discreetly made my way down the ladder, and since no screaming arose, I guess I remained undetected. I took the measurements at another time and put the pane in place like a professional glazier.

Renting an office to a gynecologist was very beneficial, because gynecology is a stable business, meaning I could be calm about the rent. This doctor delivered my second son, Arthur, while I was present—a tremendous experience for me as a father. Despite some sacrifices and saving, Ewa and I always found time and money to travel around America and visit interesting places. One of these unforgettable experiences was a family trip the three of us took to South Dakota.

There we saw the famous Mt. Rushmore, where the heads of four great American presidents have been carved into the rocky slopes of the mountains. One of the creators of this monument was a Polish sculptor, Ziółkowski. He is also the one who started work on the largest sculpture in the world, the famous Crazy Horse, carved into the rock by bulldozers.

During the same trip, we visited the one-of-a-kind Mitchell Corn Palace. It is a building decorated with all kinds of crops that are grown on the ground. Until I saw it with my own eyes, I couldn't imagine that something similar could be done! We also got to visit the Badlands, a hundred-kilometer belt of sand, rocks, and craters, reminiscent of a lunar landscape. I've got a lot of slides from this South Dakota trip.

Many wealthy Indians live in the mountains of South Dakota. Coal deposits were discovered on their territory, and thanks to this, the entire tribe became richer. In addition, there is no state law against gambling in the reservations, so Indians can get a lot of profit from casinos. They also receive federal benefits, the so-called welfare.

There are great grottos in the South Dakota mountains. We walked two kilometers deep underground, admiring the improbable shapes of the stalactites in the electric light. It seemed strange to me that nature could create something that is a true work of art. The underground walk exhausted me a lot because I had to carry a sleeping baby in my arms, but it was worth it!

Another time, we went to Indianapolis as a family. We saw the famous Indianapolis 500 there. It was a unique round of the CART PPG Indy Car World Series in which the cars exceeded 300 km/h. At such a pace, tragedies were not rare. In one of the previous races, a car left the track at a curve, killing five spectators. When we were in Indianapolis, the turns were already secured with steel railings.

The race we attended was won by a driver from Texas, a famous veteran of the steering wheel, A. J. Foyt. Although he did not complete the full distance of the race, he was in the lead when the competition was suspended due to rain. The regulations said that in such a situation, the leader becomes the winner.

From Indianapolis, we drove all night to Niagara Falls. We drove up to the waterfall itself. Masses of foaming water pouring into the abyss create a sight so amazing that I understand why Niagara is considered one of the wonders of the world. Later, dressed in hooded waterproof coats that protected us from the famous eternal rain, we went on a boat that took us to the foot of the waterfall. It was an unforgettable experience. All the participants of the cruise had wet but smiling faces. America is a beautiful country, a country of enormous opportunities.

We decided to visit Canada, as the ridge was right there and it was possible to reach it on foot. No documents were required to cross it, but guided by my intuition, I asked the guards about the legality of this undertaking. It's good that I asked! As it turned out, as I did not have an American green card, after crossing the border, I would not have had the right to return. Fortunately, I saved myself from incredible troubles. Well, the one who asks does not lose.

When the renovation of the house was finished and everything looked as it should, I received a card from the real estate agency in which they offered me a free quote. The estimate exceeded my wildest expectations: $55,000! I decided to sell immediately. I did so too. A Polish family bought my house, and I earned $20,000 on the transaction.

To trade real estate, you need some knowledge of the subject and the market. A few questions should be answered: What will the area be like in two to three years? Is it possible to somehow increase the value of the house? What are the chances of getting a loan? As a rule, the loan was 80 percent of the value of the house (i.e., I had to pay 20 percent of the value out of my pocket as a down payment, and only then could I apply for a loan from the bank. There was no problem with that, as long as I had a steady job and "good credit." After I successfully financed my first transaction, I decided that this time I would buy a bigger house so that I could live in it and do some business from it at the same time.

Every nationality in America has its business specialization: the Greeks, Italians, and French run restaurants, Germans run deli shops, and Poles run tavern-type bars where drinks and simple snacks are served.

In American cities, taverns are located on almost every corner. People come there after work to meet, chat and watch TV over a drink, or play a pool (American billiards). Americans are passionate about watching sports, which is why sports stars earn millions of dollars a year.

My real-estate agent informed me that there was a three-apartment building with a tavern for sale nearby. It was being sold by a Polish woman who already had two taverns and could not cope with them. I knew the area and its housing prices, so I was interested in this offer. I knew that the tavern business might not work out, but the profit from the rent would pay for the debts anyway. Most importantly, the price of the house was not excessive. It created an opportunity to sell the house in a few years. After some exchanges, we agreed with a Pole for $76,000.

One day, I sold one house and bought another. I covered the difference thanks to a loan from a Ukrainian bank. Other banks refused me, saying the tavern was too risky a business. I was introduced to this Ukrainian bank by a certain Ukrainian woman I know—who speaks Polish, by the way. The Ukrainians show strong national solidarity in the United States. When the last Poles left, this was not the best district; they were left defending the area from total devastation.

The purchase of an apartment building with a bar opened a new chapter in my life. I had a lot of new things to learn now. First I had to determine how to get a license to sell alcohol; such licenses are reserved by law exclusively for Americans, and therefore I could not yet obtain one.

It turned out that I could bypass this requirement by setting up a corporation. A corporation could obtain a license if its members were morally clean (i.e., did not belong to the Mafia, did not have criminal records, and had no dealings with drugs). I set up the corporation myself, without the help of lawyers. I was proud of this, because even Americans consult lawyers on such matters. I saved at least $1,000 by doing so.

I applied for a license to sell alcohol and was called by the police a few days later. I went to the police station with Ewa because she was listed in the paperwork as the secretary of our corporation. There was a requirement for the corporation to have a president and secretary. We'd had to fill these positions together. We called the corporation Wars and Sawa, which caused some problems with pronunciation among Americans.

The policeman we met with asked a lot of questions. Most of all, he was interested in where I had gotten the money to buy a house. It seemed to be about whether or not I was connected with the Mafia as the alleged owner of the bar. I had copies of all the checks for my engineering income. It took a few days for the police to check me out. Finally I got a license.

Unfortunately, before I opened the bar, I had to make a few plumbing modifications and refurbish the premises, for such requirements were set by the sanitation commission. I hired a team of Poles and Americans, who got the job done in less than a week.

My bar had a different style and better atmosphere than typical bars in Poland. In a way, it had the character of a club, and that's why I named it Ewa's Club in honor of my wife. Behind the bar I put Karen, an employee of the previous owner. She was a middle-aged American and knew how to attract an American clientele. Unfortunately, she cheated me. It is known that a dishonest bartender can "hit the owner in an hour, and even for a hundred dollars."

I waited for the opening ceremony—a kind of promotion of the place where customers can eat and drink at the expense of the company—and fired Karen shortly after. After that, my Ewa stood behind the bar, taking turns with another Polish woman.

I was watching the deal while working on engineering contracts all the time. As a rule, such a contract lasted from three to twelve months and concluded with the help of a specialized agency. The wages were much higher than for a permanent job, but I had no insurance and was not entitled to paid vacation.

All placement agencies soon had my résumé; when one contract was running out, I was already being offered another one. Most often, the new one was more favorable. And during the downtime, if my current earnings would allow it, I would take my family for a vacation of several months.

In the busy atmosphere, especially my job, our marriage began to deteriorate. It improved between us when our second son, Arthur, was born, but then problems arose again. First of all, who was supposed to look after the children? My mother-in-law stopped tending to them, hiring a nanny instead. Worse, she did this overnight. Ewa, who was employed as a secretary at the Polish Insurance Company (ONA), had to lie over the phone, stating that she was sick and could not go to work. Happily, My mother soon arrived in the States, and she took care of the boys. Unfortunately, at that time our marital conflicts had intensified.

But let's go back to the solemn opening of the bar. I invited all my Polish and American friends to participate. So many people came that there was no room to stand. One person was rubbing against the other. And because of the jostling, the situation caused a bit of conflict.

Americans are not prone to fighting. This is in part due to the law; in the States, you can say to anyone what you like, and the court will dismiss anyone's complaint because there is freedom of speech. But when you hit someone or otherwise violate someone's inviolability, it's over for you! You can't get over your compensation payments.

Before a fight takes place, there is usually a lot of chatter. Most often there is just chatter, and the feuds die out. But when people start hitting, they will do so hard with anything they can get hold of. This mainly happens to those who have nothing that can be legally seized for damages.

I think that American liberalism accepts violence, criminals, and street gangs, which hurts society as a whole. At the opening of my bar, there was a scuffle between two Americans. After a while, one of them went to a car and came back armed with a baseball bat. I understood that it was not a joke, and my friend and I took him out to the street. There I told him to go home. Fortunately, he obeyed.

The second unpleasant thing about this party was the envy I sensed from some compatriots. "I thought that you bought a place for three hundred people, but only sixty people can enter here," said a Polish friend of mine, whom I invited with his wife. He envied me because I was pushing forward so quickly financially, and he could not help but make a bitter remark.

After the ceremonial opening, everyday bar life began. Little by little, I figured out about procurement and taxes, and most of all, I was learning the mentality of my clientele. So far, it was almost exclusively American, even though the bar was located not far from the center of the Polish Quarter, or Belmont, Puławski, and Milwaukee.

There was a nice, social atmosphere in the tavern. Regular customers met at my place every day. For the young people who came in, I put a new stereo in the tavern. They listened to their favorite rock music, and they quickly began calling the tavern "Rock-Bar."

These young people were smoking marijuana in the street. They only came into the bar for drinks. Of course, I did not allow smoking of joints inside and rejected all proposals to smoke with them. I knew that I had to be strict in this respect, because I could easily lose my license by allowing pot on the premises. Besides, I was an opponent of marijuana, as I had seen what this supposedly innocent drug could do to people. Marijuana smokers are always excited, hot-tempered, and pointlessly talkative. Their brains are no longer working properly. And now and then I heard nonsensical conversations: "Shouldn't marijuana be introduced to pharmacies as medicine?"

And it happened. The post-war hippie generation, in California and Arizona, approved marijuana as a medicine in the November 1996 election. The state law in these places is in opposition to federal law.

Chicago's taverns were spaced approximately every one hundred meters, so the competition was fierce. To attract customers, different promotions were used, such as the so-called happy hour between 3:00 p.m. and 5:00 p.m., when a pint was twenty-five cents instead of the normal dollar. I also extended the open hours of the tavern, sometimes even to 2:00 a.m. Unfortunately, my license allowed the bar to operate only until this hour. Some taverns closed at 4:00 a.m.

It was hard work. There was always something going on. The patrons stole beer, they got into fights, and, finally, a drunk customer attacked my mother with a knife. Though I was often tired after working in the office, I often had to wake up to separate fighting bullies. The worst thing was that I couldn't count on the police. Whenever I summoned them, instead of intervening, they would check my license.

But there were also anecdotal cases. For example, a group of several Poles who all worked illegally and lived together in a three-room apartment frequented the bar. Their visas has long expired, but of course they didn't intend to leave the States. They made good money, but they spent most of their income in the tavern, especially on Friday evenings. They said they drank their sorrow to Poland, to their families. The leader in this was a certain Roman, who often lost money while drunk. My mother, who served in the bar, once found a hundred-dollar bill left by Roman and gave it back the next day when he sobered up.

One day our Poles were having fun until late hours. Luckily, a certain lady with a dog entered the tavern. Roman bought her a drink, and they left the bar together. Of course, he took her to the apartment where his friends were sleeping, hence the whole thing gained publicity.

When Roman started to have sex with the woman, the dog, thinking that she was hurt, jumped on his ass. The dog received a kick, of course, and this is where the drama began. In the United States, animals are treated as family members, and they are even buried in special cemeteries. Damulka went mad and called the police. What happened next is easy to guess the policemen identified Roman and the other Poles, and then, having declared their visas invalid, they referred the case to the US Immigration and Naturalization Service.

The procedure in such cases is simple: the offender must pay a deposit of $3,000 guaranteeing that he will leave the United States within three months. Some of the heroes of this anecdote left on time and regained their bail; others stayed and probably worked illegally somewhere. This is how the cheerful Roman messed up his and his friends' lives.

Today there is a constant game going on between US Immigration and Customs Enforcement (ICE) and undocumented non-citizens. There are constant hunts at workplaces. It looks like the ICE officers enter through one door and the illegally employed undocumented workers run through the other. The powerlessness of the authorities is proved by statistical data. For example, the population of newcomers from Central and South America has increased by 40 percent in recent years. It has even gotten to the point that in some parts of the country, Spanish is now unofficially a second language.

English is not an official language in the United States. It sounds paradoxical, but unfortunately, it is true. For immigrants to preserve their national cultures, American liberals did not declare English an official language, and there are currently about two hundred languages spoken in the United States. This is not good for the children of immigrants, which is especially noticeable among immigrants from Mexico. Republicans are trying to change the order of things and declare English the official language, as well as prohibit the burning of the American flag.

The situation between me and Ewa had deteriorated to such an extent that we decided to get a divorce. The divorce meant the loss of everything for me, because when the property was divided, the court ruled that Ewa deserved almost everything and I deserved a fig with poppy seeds. American law strongly favors women, which increases the divorce rate, to the detriment of families. Fathers are simply thrown out of their homes. This has led to enormous chaos in American society. Welfare does not pay if the man is at home. Marriages pay, as if "marriage tribute", additional taxes. A woman can call the police on any pretext for a row, including lying about threats, and her male partner can be thrown into the street from his own house.

I experienced this myself when Ewa prepared a lie. As a result of this social situation in the USA, 11 million children are brought up without a father. They are devoid of paternal care and discipline, and are educationally unattended. There is an opinion among women that a father is the best when at a distance and he sends a check regularly; the law also holds this position. This is a bad solution. America is already talking about it. It will take a long time to fix this. I lost my children in one hour when Ewa came with a policeman and took them, and I had raised them alone for nine years. Her statement that I was a better father than she was a mother was not enough. Luckily my boys had a good foundation, and she couldn't hurt them much.

Many women simply hunt wealthy guys, then act on any excuse to get divorced. And lawyers, mainly Jewish ones who are known to have no qualms about it, earn the most. Two such lawyers were hired by Ewa. They robbed me. I have to call it that, because I paid them for her service, but at the same time they tricked her into paying a fee of $1,300. Thanks to this advocate's insolence, there was a temporary ceasefire between Ewa and me; for a moment she forgot about her injury and asked me to help her get the money back. Then our relations improved. I mean, divorce did us good. And I sued the lawyers and their union, and they had to pay the money back.

Unfortunately, I also encountered a similar case of meanness from my fellow countryman and my engineer colleague. The two of us established a professional partnership to act as a company toward our employers and not to pay tribute to various agencies at the same time. It was unfortunate that we got employed in two plants—me on a contract, and my colleague in a permanent position. I have already mentioned that contract engineers earn more, and this was also the case here. I was paid twenty dollars an hour, which was a lot for Chicago, and he only twelve dollars an hour. Of course, he started to be envious and then demanded that I withdraw from the company. But why should I withdraw if the company was increasing my income? Ultimately, my colleague went so far as to blackmail me: he threatened to smear me in front of my manager. Indeed, I lost my job shortly after, and I suspect this was thanks to my partner. Well, as my grandfather used to say, "The swallows used to say that partners are not good." This adage was not, coincidentally, created in Poland; I am afraid that we, Poles really have problems with understanding and implementing company business. But it is simple: you let me make some money, I let you make money. In any case, I support Polish business in America and I advise other Poles about this.

The formation of corporations in the USA, Japan, and Germany only happened because people generally trusted each other. Young Polish capitalists should know about this; as long as people don't trust each other, no big domestic business will arise!

Before the divorce, my earnings and expenses were quite orderly: rent made it possible to pay off my bank loan, income from the tavern (60 percent of gross turnover) allowed me to support my family decently, and what I earned on contracts was reflected in future investments.

I note at this point that few people in America are saving. The average American lives, as the saying goes, from paycheck to paycheck; that is, what one earns, one spends. The exception to this rule is Asian Americans, who save up to 30 percent of their earnings. Poles save less, only 20 percent of their earnings, but that is still more than Americans, who spend 90 percent of their income on current expenses. The reluctance to save is one of the shortcomings of the American economy, and this can be seen especially in times of recession. At such times, people who are paying for things in installments and have no savings lose their property. The word "foreclosure" is very popular in the United States.

After the divorce, the tavern went to Ewa, but she could not manage the business herself. The bar quickly fell into disrepair, and there was no money to buy a new license. Ewa wanted to give the house and tavern back to the city in exchange for a college scholarship, but I put this ridiculous idea out of her mind. She asked me for help. I took over the management of the bar again and at the same time announced an offers to sell. We both wanted to sell it and get out of the eatery business.

But it was not easy, and the swing in sales lasted two years. Finally I found a Polish couple willing to buy. But they had no money. I gave them a loan of 12 percent, which they promised to pay back within three years. In the role of a bank, I was relieved of my obligation because the banks officially refused to grant them a loan. I shared the money with Ewa, and we were relieved that the trouble was gone.

I enrolled Roger in elementary school when he was five, a year earlier than required by law. Until then, he had spoken only Polish, and now he had to learn English quickly. To my surprise, after a month he began to read fluently. Soon after, the teacher assigned him as an interpreter to another Polish boy who had just been admitted to the school.

There was initially a friendship between Roger and this boy, but then Roger began to avoid him.

"Why are you avoiding this friend?" I asked him.

"Because the boys are calling us Poles," he explained.

I gave him a lecture, telling him that the word "Pole" is not an insult and that he should be proud of his Polish origin, because Poland had a thousand-year-old culture (i.e., five times older than the United States). Unfortunately, I am not sure whether I convinced him. I can only believe that there will come a day when Roger will feel proud of his origin. Roger was not an angel. He spent a lot of time on the street and played with the inappropriate company.

In a city like Chicago, it's hard to keep a child from doing this. I remember very well how an older friend pushed him into a pile of snow and held him there until Roger got frostbite. I then intervened with the police in the juvenile department and made sure that the father of the bully paid me for the costs of the treatment. I hope that when he coughed the money up, he cut himself out of anger.

Roger also committed various pranks. He broke a car window and set fire to some newspapers under the neighbor's gate. I tried to temper similar impulses and raise my son according to the traditional discipline that I remembered from my own home. On the other hand, Ewa was a supporter of liberal methods fashionable in America, which are already known to result in disastrous educational effects. Roger graduated from a good private Catholic high school and entered the University of Santa Barbara in 1993.

The home, corporation, and bar were sold for $112,000. We were to receive $56,000 more in return for the loan granted to the buyers. I had realized my plan. I earned a good sum on the real estate and the business I had been running for years, plus the income from my rent had allowed me to live well. At the same time, I avoided the greatest risk posed by running a bar; namely, I did not develop alcoholism. Many tavern and bar owners drink up because they have the best alcohol on hand, and it's free. The customers also tempt them by often proposing that they have a drink together. They can even take offense when the owners refuse. Maybe I'm an unusual Pole, but I've never been drunk in my life. I just have a kind of alarm system in my head that alerts me: "Stop, not one more." This came in handy when running the tavern.

I was planning a trip to Houston, Texas, where I was expecting to get a job. Before I left, I bought a travel trailer that could sleep six people with all the comforts. I pulled the trailer with a Ford Van.

I packed my things and, together with my mother and children, set off for Texas. We had all sorts of adventures along the way. It turned out the trailer didn't have a good connection to the lights and we couldn't drive at night. I stopped by the road, and we stayed overnight in the trailer until the first rays of the sun appeared. We arrived at Houston after two arduous days of driving through the prairie and desert. I parked the trailer at a campground in the eastern part of the city.

At the same time, I started looking for a job and a house where I could comfortably live with my family and which would be an investment. The new state, new neighborhood, and new customs in a sense meant that I had to learn America from scratch.

I noticed that it is not as easy for an immigrant to break through here as in Chicago, because Texas simply has fewer immigrants and hence there are greater prejudices on the part of employers. To make matters worse, the so-called oil recession was starting, and Texas, which had so far prospered because of oil production, began to run into economic trouble. People were losing their jobs, and hence their homes, as they were unable to pay their mortgages. I didn't think the recession would last that long in Texas, and having had enough of the four of us in the trailer, I started looking to buy a house.

While touring with a real estate agent in the area, I came across an opportunity. The house was large but neglected, and its owners were just getting divorced. This, of course, had an impact on the price, which, as the house was in the northwest part of the Houston suburbs—a nice neighborhood—was quite low. Similar houses in the neighborhood cost $80,000, and I made an offer for $60,000 and finally bought for $65,000. I was unemployed, I had to make a large down payment, as much as $37,000, and the bank agreed to loan the rest of the sum at a fairly low percentage, only 7.8 percent. I must add that there were also houses and estates worth $300,000 in these parts, where wealthy people who kept horses lived. So I followed the good old investment rule; I bought the cheapest house in the most expensive district.

I was now the owner of a ten-room house with a yard so large that one could play golf on it, but I still had no job. Out of boredom, I got a job with a Baptist neighbor who ran a tree-cutting business. I was earning six dollars an hour, and the job was tough. After all, it is not so easy to cut down a large oak growing right next to a house, so as not to damage the building. I did not damage any buildings, but I nearly lost my life when a certain Ed who worked with me dropped a log weighing twenty kilograms near me. He was still so brazen that after this incident that he said, "Be careful that you don't have a severe headache!"

Having decided that it was not worth risking my life for a lame few dollars, I said good-bye to my career as a lumberjack. I treated this work as physical entertainment to rebuild myself mentally.

I was able to find out that the people of Texas had a different temperament than the people of the North. One day I heard a violent pounding on the door. I opened it, and there was my neighbor, Bochnian—Czech by descent, but typically Texan in terms of mentality.

"Put your shoes on and go outside," he said to me. "We will fight!" It turned out that my four-year-old son had hit his five-year-old daughter. Had it not been for another, saner, neighbor who spoke to him in time to get him to understand, it would have gone from childhood quarrels to a clash between fathers. Texans are like that, though not all of them, as the mediator assured me. Half an hour after the incident, Bochnian visited me with a bottle of whiskey. I think the hot temperaments of Texans are influenced by hot climate.

The sun in Houston is so sharp that we Europeans should not sunbathe in it. Having lived for twelve years in the so-called Sunbelt, I have learned to avoid the sun, because it dries out and damages the skin and causes wrinkles. This is the truth that is finally talked about, and there are warnings against excessive sunbathing.

When I came to Houston, I was not warned about spending hours in the sun. After showering and wiping myself with a towel one day, I broke a mole on my skin, which was red from being in the sun. I drove a big Yamaha 650 motorcycle to a hospital fifty kilometers away from my house. After quite a long wait, the surgeon saw me and offered to the mole, which was the size of a penny, from my hand. I agreed without hesitation. The operation lasted thirty minutes, and then I was free. The surgeon applied a few stitches and a large dressing to the operation site.

When the anesthesia stopped working, the pain got worse and worse. I barely made it home, my teeth clenched. I felt like a hero driving that fifty kilometers while exposed to the dangers of high-speed traffic on the Houston freeways.

Fulfilling my sons' request, the next day I took them to the pool. Roger was seven years old then, and Arthur was five years old. They both could swim already. I taught them to avoid unpleasant surprises, but I was always around anyhow. After jumping into the water at a depth of three meters, Arthur got water under his goggles. Frightened, he lost his bearings and began to drown!

The lifeguard girl next to the lifeguard tower where I was standing was facing the other way at that moment. With the instinct of a lifeguard, I jumped into the water and pulled my son ashore. The wound on my neck began to bleed from contact with the water. I had to go to the hospital for cleaning and disinfection. Fortunately, there is almost no trace of that adventure. Only memories are left.

During my stay in Houston, I got a message from Ewa about the death of my friend Janusz. He died in a car accident, and the tragic end to his American escapade is worth telling. It is an example of how a Pole can fail in the United States. Janusz did not get along from the very beginning. It was I who brought him to America, and I helped him as much as I could, but as you know, in the end, a man can only help himself, and poor Janusz could not do that. Unable to learn new activities quickly, he lost his jobs all the time. He lived with me for a long time, not paying, but only helping with minor home repairs.

I also hired him in a tiny business I started, which involved hauling broken cars into my garage and repairing them. I paid Janusz $200 a week in cash, and the business didn't do well.

Janusz's death shocked me. We had experienced a lot together in our youth, and we were friends, so I took it upon myself to send the body to Poland. Not knowing what formalities it required, I called the Polish consulate. It cost $4,000 to ship the coffin home, and the consulate couldn't help me there. I called Janusz's wife about the tragedy by phone and asked whether I could send the cremated body. She agreed with great sadness.

At the funeral home, I was asked to confirm the identity of the body. Yes, it was Janusz—a long face with sharp features carved in stone. His muscular, almost wiry build showed that he had worked a lot in his young life—unfortunately in vain.

Once upon a time, his muscular physique was featured on the covers of the bodybuilding magazine *Sport for All*. I shipped all of Janusz's American assets by sea via a Polish shipping company. I wanted to send the urn with the ashes packed in a parcel by airmail, but the clerk informed me that I would have to obtain a permit from the Polish consulate to do so. I did so simply by sending the consulate a check for $170.

At that moment, I was reminded of the horror I had witnessed while still in Italy. A Polish immigrant died there, and his colleagues, not wanting to pay for the formalities, sent his ashes in a coffee can.

The recession in Texas was deepening, and there was no hope of improvement. I started thinking about going to California. That had been my intention from the very beginning, as soon as I was in the States, but I was always held back by some fear. I didn't know whether I would find a job, and the houses were the most expensive there.

Here in Houston, I was set up. I had a place to live, and the children went to the local school. I didn't want to make them feel insecure and decided to leave them alone at first. I knew California only from my vacations there while I was still living in Chicago. Now my going there was not supposed to be a vacation, but a serious attempt to settle down there permanently.

I rented my first apartment in Hollywood. The district is not very special. I am not a racist, but somehow it happens that wherever Black people live, there is generally terrible filth. I cannot find a more complimentary term for it; it is just crap. I had a very nice apartment with two bedrooms. It was located next to the motel and belonged to its owner. The price of $450 a month included furniture, linen changes, and the use of the pool. I lived near Hollywood Boulevard, where the famous stars are imbedded in the sidewalk. I was walking alone around these stars and nearby bars, pondering what to do with myself.

On Fridays and Saturdays, I watched the performances of amateur artists in the area of the Chinese theater, and so my time was running low. It was said to be a dangerous neighborhood, but I didn't have this feeling.

I had two job opportunities, one in South Arabia and one in Santa Barbara. Not wanting to leave the States, I decided to take the second option. I started working at Archer-Spencer. At the outset, the boss invited me to lunch and showed me the city.

One of the most interesting monuments in Santa Barbara is the two-hundred-year-old Spanish convent cathedral. California was Spanish for a long time, then it became a territory of Mexico, and then the Americans won it. The story is not as long as those of European countries, but it is also interesting. The Iberian character of the architecture testifies to the past of Spanish Santa Barbara . The buildings are cream colored, and the presence of palm trees on the streets gives the city a bright goodness and nice color.

For the next few years, Santa Barbara was my home.

I rented a room in the suburbs with three Americans. Each one had a separate bedroom, and the two lounges were shared: one for me and my American neighbor, the other for two American girls. We also had a pool and Jacuzzi.

The kitchen was shared, which I did not approve of, as my neighbors were very messy and often kept unwashed dishes in the sink for so long they started to stink. The guy I was living with ran a restaurant but was going through bankruptcy. He lost everything, so he was forced to live as a roommate. He started working as a cook, as he didn't have enough to cover the rent.

The girls had their own lives, and we only exchanged smiles and said hi in greeting to greet them. The owner lived nearby in his own house with his family. He had children, so he complained that the tenants bathed naked in the morning. But that was the style there: freedom of opinion and relaxed manners.

The millionaires' district of Hope Ranch was nearby. Big, beautiful houses on large pieces of mountainous land overlooked the ocean. There were also private beaches here and there, only for residents. The public beach, called Henry Beach, to which one could descend straight from the mountains, was also very beautiful. I could walk for hours on the sand at the edge of the undulating ocean, contemplating the future. I've always been an optimist, and now, too, hope never left me.

I used to call my mom and kids a lot in Texas. Winter holidays were approaching, and Texas was cold, especially at night. Mom complained that the boys were mischievous and she couldn't cope with them. I had decided to take them to California. However, where I lived, we would not all have room.

I had to find a place where my children would be accepted, as well as my German shepherd named Bear and a trailer—in a word, the whole family. I found a small summer house on the beach at Rincon Point. It was a modest place but was surrounded by very expensive houses. It was waiting for its turn to be demolished because there were plans to build houses worth $700,000 here. These plans were implemented after two years, and so far I had been paying $150 a month for the use of the house and was saving money to buy my own house.

I was transporting my family to California for adventures. When we passed Austin, Texas, there was a glass on the road. It was only because of my racing skills that I managed to keep control of the car and trailer to avoid an accident. We had to stay at the hotel, and it wasn't until the next night that I went down to my beach house with my family.

I enrolled my children in school in Carpenteria. Close contact with nature made them feel as if they were in California on vacation. At night, we were lulled to sleep by the sound of the ocean, and during the day we could walk for hours on the beach. The only problem was the lack of running water, for which I had to drive to a nearby park. We took showers at the YMCA sports club.

Mom started to complain a little. She laughed that I was around forty years old and lived like a teenager on vacation. The time had come to find a decent home to live in, especially since the Chicago apartment house had been fully paid for. The people who bought that house from us wanted to sell it. They had to take out a new loan to pay off our temporary loan. We shared about $60,000 dollars with Ewa.

Ewa asked me to help her invest this sum. She had caught this bug from me. She put forward a proposal that I should buy a house with her as a partnership. I had undertaken quite a few such ventures in my marriage, and I had not done well. I said that I could help her find a good investment, but with her already home, I did not want to buy.

Her school friend, an American of Polish descent, came to Ewa. He did not speak Polish because it was his grandfather who had come to America. Later I found out that he had a platonic love for Ewa. His name was John, and he helped Ewa get through the last year of her studies. She had gotten through her first two years of study with my help, and I wanted her to cope on her own. He willingly agreed to Ewa's proposal to buy the house together, especially since he was already working.

I started looking for homes for them and myself. It took several weekends to do research on the offers on the market. I arranged for Ewa to be hire a fictitious beautician, as otherwise they would not be eligible for a loan.

At the same time, my offer was accepted for a nice, big house in Goleta for $162,000, and their offer of $150,000 was accepted for a house in Montecito. Their neighborhood was better, but the house was smaller and expandable. I told them exactly what to do to significantly increase the value of the home. Fortunately, I didn't have to do anything with mine. After five years, after they built the house according to my instructions, the value of the house jumped to $600,000, and the value of my house went up to $300,000 without any investment. That was my last gift for my ex-wife.

It's good that I didn't have to live with Ewa and go through that hell again. Money is often not the most important thing.

We moved to a new house in Goleta, a seaside resort town adjacent to the north of Santa Barbara. Our house had nine large rooms, a fireplace, a large bar, a pool table, a solarium on the roof, and a Jacuzzi in the garden. This place was especially suited to games and parties. Thirty plump, exotic fruit trees grew in the garden, and it was only a five-minute drive to the beach. I liked this place a lot.

I started working in a local Polish organization called the Polish-American Art Association, which promoted Polish culture in the United States and supported freedom movements in the country. After some time, I was unanimously elected president. The Polish community from Santa Barbara is an aristocracy among the Polish community. Many of its members have been living in the United States for thirty to forty years. They speak Polish well and are keenly interested in Polish affairs. I organized lectures, films, and slide shows for them, as well as theater and cabaret performances. I conducted meetings in two languages because there were members who did not know Polish but who felt Polish in some sense.

We organized trade in second-hand goods, and in this way we collected tens of thousands of dollars. We sent aid to Solidarity in Poland, as well as to Polish hospitals and church charities. We also helped Poles in Paris who were unable to pay the costs of treatment, and we financed operations for people coming to the States from the country.

I was unemployed for a while and my time to take additional vocational exams as a so-called engineer in training, as well as the real estate licensing exam. Many Poles benefited from my advice as a broker, including my ex-wife, Ewa, whom I advised on an exceptionally profitable investment. However, not everyone was grateful. There was a case when a client—a Pole who, thanks to my professional advice, earned $140,000, almost wanted to sue me for $150 because he noticed that in the house he had bought, the toilet bowl was broken.

I also had a lot of trouble selling my own home in Texas. Eventually, a certain Jew bought it. He paid $2,500, and that was it. Months passed, and no installments were received from him. Living in California, I had to act through an attorney. He conducted the so-called foreclosure, or legal removal of the house, but to physically collect the house, I had to drive my car across half of America.

When I got to the Enchanted Valley estate, where my unfortunate property was located, Jay (the buyer) could see me through the window, but he didn't open it for a long time. Then I realized that he needed a delay to notify the police.

He had a deal with the local captain to protect him from me. Just after talking to Jay (politely, by the way) I got into the car and unfolded my map, and a police car appeared. The cops accused me of harassing Jay and told me to stay away from his—*my*—house! It got to the point where I had to live outside of Houston and pursue my case from there. US law protects the owner, and until I finally won the trial, that was Jay.

The process was protracted. At the first hearing, the judge adjourned the case for a week because I appeared alone, without a lawyer. There is no such law stating that I must necessarily use a lawyer, but the professional solidarity of lawyers has worked. The judge wanted his lawyer to earn.

This cost me $300. (Most attorneys paid under a thousand

dollars don't lift a finger .) I won the case! Jay and his family had to leave in five days.

I was afraid of visiting the house again at the last minute, and I watched the house with anxiety. When I saw that he was packing for departure, I went and asked for the keys to be returned. Then he fell into a rage and ran to his neighbor (the one who once wanted to fight me), asking him to lend him a rifle. Without waiting for things to develop, I quickly drove away, and when I showed up the next day, the house was empty. Few times in my life have I felt this kind of relief!

At this point, it is worth mentioning an adventure I experienced. After a hot day, it was nice to relax with a cocktail in front of the TV in the air-conditioned room of the house. For my colleague Andrzej M. (whom I helped get to America), everything was new, and I tried to show him as much as possible. I did not predict the events we experienced one evening. Andrzej M., as an intern, spent four years in a correctional facility of the Ministry of the Interior, on Rakowiecka Street. I met him in a café on the day on which he was released.

He, as a chemical engineer and I, as an electrical engineer, started working at FSO. We knew the nature of socializing. I felt pity for him and therefore agreed to help him and brought him to Houston, Texas, where I was currently staying.

We were sitting in this house in the evening and chatting with my mother when someone knocked on the front door. In America, people are reluctant to open the door to strangers who knock at night, and certainly to let them into the house. I opened the door, and there was a man in the doorway who asked me to use the phone. I didn't ask questions. Thinking his car must have broken down, I let him in. He called his father and in a trembling voice begged him to answer him, but received a negative reply. Through the window, in the darkness of the night, I saw the police with flashlights in my yard. I looked out into the street saw a few policemen on horses stopped in front of my house. I guessed that the police were looking for the man who was at my house.

My mother and my friend Andrzej sat in fear and silence. I told this man to leave my house. He pleaded, saying that he could not leave the house because the police might shoot him. I'd heard about incidents where the Texas police killed criminals without provocation in certain situations. This man asked the police to detain him in my presence, as if it would provide him with some safety. I opened the front door, the policeman asked whether the man they were looking for was here. I opened the door wide, and they saw the wanted man in the long hall. Several policemen burst in, grabbed the individual, and knocked him facedown to the floor. One put handcuffs on him, and the other quickly took off his high cowboy boots in search of a pistol. Fortunately, no gun was found, and they took him to the car with his socks on. While he was leaving, one of the policemen asked what he had been doing here. I replied that he had wanted to use the phone, and that was the end of the conversation.

The next day, I read in the local newspaper that a man who had been paroled and suspected of murdering his girlfriend had been caught in our neighborhood. The newspaper also reported that a gun had been found in our forest. By accident, I got involved in a local criminal scandal. I learned that this man first knocked on the door of our neighbors, and they refused to open it. Maybe I still have European safety habits!

I lived in Houston for a while, working on a contract in Krenko, where I was designing control systems for industrial cranes. When the contract was finished, I thought there was no point in my further staying in Texas. I finally decided to tie things up in California. While in California, I had received an official letter from the IRS that my tax return was missing an item of $44,000 in cash that and I owed $16,000 with interest and penalties.

I didn't know what $44,000 in cash they were talking about,

and I disregarded the matter, hoping that they would send another letter with some explanation. Bad luck—all the other letters came in while I was away from California. The next year, the sum of the debt grew so large that a bailiff unexpectedly came, threatening me with seizure and sale of my house against the debt. I got a tax attorney (he charged $1,000 for the case). The next year, I had an overpayment of $5,000 and was hoping to get it back, but with that $44,000 pending, the IRS held my return. This case dragged on for three years, and the debt grew, reaching around $20,000.

I started going through my passport in the office and looking at the dates from 1988 when I was suspected of having these currency transactions. I saw that I was in Poland at that time,and I immediately realized what had happened. Before coming to Poland, I was to enter a transit camp in Bathen, Germany, to complete the formalities for my friend Andrzej M. and his wife, who was still in Warsaw at that time. Thinking I might buy a Mercedes in Germany, I took $22,000 from a bank in Houston. The dollar was low at the time, and it would take a lot of effort to bring a Mercedes to America, so in Germany, I decided not to buy it. I wandered with this packet of money through the rest of my journey.

At the border, the Polish customs officer to whom I showed the money wanted a gift because she thought that the money came from some smuggling. I was afraid to part with this package in Poland. I brought this money back to Houston and deposited it back into the same bank I had taken it from. The bank is required to report any such major transaction to the IRS. So they reported two transactions, each for $22,000, which was where the cash turnover of $44,000 came from. The case was clarified, and the IRS canceled the debt and returned the retained money, which does not mean that they returned a lawyer fee or several years of trouble.

After many weeks of browsing through advertisements in the

Santa Barbara News-Press and *Los Angeles Times* and sending out nearly a hundred résumés, I was hired by Fluor Daniel, one of the major engineering firms in America. The interview was conducted by five management guys with me. That is understandable, because a place of such renown cannot afford to hire just anyone. They take only the best and pay them accordingly. I received a salary of $44,000 a year to start with.

Fluor Daniel is located in the city of Irvine in Orange County and occupies a complex of dark glass buildings that are architecturally interconnected. Outside there are lawns, fountains, and a huge area, and inside there are paintings, bas-reliefs, escalators, high-speed elevators, and an elegant café. And no wonder, since the company has built industry practically all over the world.

Colleagues told me that in their heyday they were driven to Los Angeles to meet customers by helicopter. They had a landing strip on the roof of the headquarters. Then, as a result of the fuel crisis, the company went into decline a bit, sold off some investments and real estate, and merged with Daniel from South Carolina. When I was working there, we specialized in Middle Eastern refineries.

I started working in the Small Industrial Projects Department, the modest name of which did not reflect the intellectual scale of the work we were performing. A house on rubber cushions was designed for the fire brigade command. Yes—a house that rests on several dozen two-meter cushions to protect it from the effects of an earthquake.

Working at Fluor Daniel was 100 percent professional and involved a lot of travel. In Bakersfield, we installed equipment for the well-known pharmaceutical company Sandoz, and again in San Diego, I did a lot of cost estimates for energy projects for naval bases. To enter the base areas, one had to have a special pass. As the owner of such a pass, I was able to see up close the power that shakes the whole world. The giant aircraft carriers had their power plants on board and used as much energy as a small city. In peacetime, they collected it from offshore substations using cables. Cable power and substations were the scope of my projects. In total, I had fifty projects to do on various bases. A lot of money was spent on it. Today the real relief for the budget is the reduction of military expenditures, which were already unnecessary to such an extent when the Soviet Union collapsed.

I had $42,000 set aside, and it was time to look around for my next house. I chose from among many possibilities a large, six-bedroom home located in an expensive and good neighborhood in Orange County called Villa Park. They wanted $450,000 for the property. I played it smart. Here I owe the reader some explanation of how to buy US property. War veterans can buy houses without any down payment on a so-called VA loan guaranteed by the US government but provided by a bank. A loan insured by the government agency FHA requires only a 3 percent down payment and also comes from a bank. There is also a third type of loan, the so-called conventional loan, which requires a 5 percent to 20 percent down payment. You must meet the relevant regulatory requirements to qualify for any of these loans. The smaller the down payment, the stricter the provisions for receiving the loan. I assumed that I would pay 20 percent of the purchase price as a down payment because such a route was the most realistic; it did not require detailed documentation of the income. I offered $400,000, and the seller agreed to $420,000. A 20 percent down payment from $420,000 is $84,000 and I had only $42,000. The question was, Where could I get the remaining $42,000? I proposed to the seller to lend me the missing $42,000 for one year at an interest rate of 12 percent. I said I would charge my second house in Goleta with a debt of $42,000 in his favor. So it was as if I had given him a part of the house in Goleta as collateral. For a whole year later, I paid him only a monthly percentage (that is [$42,000 × 0.12] / 12 = $420). The seller agreed to the offer, I confirmed it, and the contract was valid.

There are also closing cost transactions that are around 2 percent. As a result, I needed $1,500 at the closing. Even though I had a 3 percent commission as a buyer's broker after closing this deal myself, I couldn't close without the missing $1,500. I applied for a loan of this $1,500 for one day from the selling broker. He said that would be no problem and he would loan me the $1,500 for the day, but for $150, which was the going rate. I had no other option, so I agreed to this deal. It was in the interest of this broker to close this transaction, as it conditioned other transactions because the seller of my house was buying another house for himself.

I soon found out what this whole intricate arrangement was about. The man who sold the house to me was not its owner but only rented it out. He had a lease contract with the right to buy the house for $370,000 . When he found me as a buyer for $420,000, he had a prospect of earning $50,000 and announced that that he was selling it just to earn money. So this was not his house, but he was selling it.

I know that until recently in Poland there was an opinion that if someone earns money this way, it is rather immoral. In America, if this is done within the law, everything is okay. The seller could confidently lend me the $42,000 at a high interest rate because that was his profit on this transaction and it was secured with my second home. Under banking laws, a down payment cannot be borrowed. Therefore, the seller also deposited his money before closing the transaction to my neutral account to the so-called escrow. Before the transaction was closed, I couldn't move.

Escrow is kind of like our notary's office in Poland. There were two transactions simultaneously. First, the seller bought the house, and then he sold it to me almost at the same time. Before the purchase was made, however, one more important element remained. I had to find a bank or mortgage company to lend me the money to buy this house. Representatives of these institutions came to my office to pick up completed loan applications. To be sure that I would receive the loan, I sent the application to five financial institutions at the same time. How important is credit, or solvency in the past? I found out the hard way. I had one unpaid bill of $28 from four years prior, and on that basis, four banks refused my loan.

A chiropractor had announced a free appointment, which I took advantage of, but later sent a bill to my home for $28. I ignored it, and he turned the debt over to a collection agency. I sent $28 to the collection agency and an explanatory letter to the bank, and eventually, the fifth bank gave me a loan. After many maneuvers, I became the owner of the estate in Southern California, in one of the most beautiful places in America. In the end, I had $84,000 in advance, and the bank gave me a loan for the remaining amount up to $420,000, or $336,000.

All of the purchase formalities took about three months. After dealing with them, I moved into my new home. The house in which I live to this day is a retreat from the crowds of everyday life. It is surrounded by mountains and lots of greenery. There are palm trees, olive trees, and a lot of fruit trees. In California, the mountains are more expensive than the plains, and suburban towns are more expensive than in the city, and of course, the most expensive is the Pacific coast, or at least the ocean view. An ocean view is said to be worth a million dollars. Teresita, my girlfriend, vacated her home and moved in with me.

This time she was my roommate, and she helped me pay my monthly debt for the mortgage. There are two major problems with owning a house in America, especially in California. The first is the buying process and the second is the ongoing payments. Paying the mortgage, tax, and insurance costs me $3,500 a month. Initially, I had roommates who helped me financially. I've been living in this house for seven years now, and I'm managing some-how; and the investment is working for me.

It has not always been easy, but you have to take some risks in business.

I knew my house was worth more than I paid for it. After a few months, I decided to refinance my house. A professional company estimated it at a new value of $525,000. The mortgage company gave me a loan of 75 percent of that amount, or $390,000, to pay off my previous debt of $336,000, and I collected about $60,000. I already had the money to pay off $42,000 in debt at the end of the year, and so I did. I never liked being in debt, and if I had to go into debt, I always paid it off on time.

Fluor Daniel had less work for me, and from doing small proj-ects, I was transferred to the Bank of America project. This bank is one of the largest in America and has thousands of branches. We installed new computers in all branches and the central building.

The central building was located in downtown Los Angeles. The ten-story building had no windows, and all of the floors had large commercial computers. The building was strictly guarded, as it was like the brains behind all of Bank of America in Southern California. Through the network, all these branches sent informa-tion about each transaction.

On the sixth floor of the building, I was waiting with my friend for the elevator when a strong earthquake started. The elevators stopped because they had antishock relays. I had experi-enced earthquakes before, but they can be felt very strongly in sky-scrapers. Recent studies have shown that Los Angeles skyscrapers will not withstand the stress of an earthquake with a magnitude of seven or eight on the Richter scale.

While on this topic, I should mention that it is unfortunate that at the time of writing this chapter, on April 20, 1994, I was working in Sylmar. It is a few miles from the epicenter of a 5.8 magnitude earthquake a few months prior, which left about fifty people dead and several highways collapsed. In our office, computers crashed to the floor. I don't think them every day, but earthquakes are an inseparable part of this beautiful corner of the earth. Thanks to earthquakes, we have beautiful mountains in California.

During earthquakes, layers of earth and rock push outwards, creating beautiful hills. Ela provided me with a gallon of drinking water, peanuts, and pretzels for my car so that when an earthquake would keep me in the car for a long time, I would have something to eat.

The next stage of my work in Fluor was the San Onofre nuclear power plant. It is located roughly in the middle between Los Angeles and San Diego. During the first month of training and the so-called security clearance, I gained 100 percent trust from management and a pass. But I didn't work there long. When I ran out of work, they gave me a temporary leave. It is always the case that the highest earners go first.

Well, I found another, better-paying job, and when my boss from Fluor asked me to come back over the phone, I made my consent conditional on a large raise. This was deemed to be arrogant, and a nasty note was been added to my file. Contract work is generally short-term. After three months of work, I sent out a résumé again in search of an opening. In difficult moments of recession, a company employing engineers can get one hundred résumés per opening.

Locally, no one was hired, and one of the agencies called to ask whether I wanted to go to the state of New Mexico on a fairly good several-month contract for $28 an hour. After a short telephone conference with the agent and the female manager of the electrical department, I was hired. They wanted me to come immediately, but I gave myself a week to prepare and travel.

I packed my van, and after one day of driving, I was there. Our facility was the only one of its kind in the world. It was forty miles from the city of Carlsbad, in the middle of the prairie. From the outside, it looked like the most modern arms factory. It was a tightly fenced facility with one entrance through the main guardhouse. There were auxiliary buildings on the surface of the earth, and a kilometer and a half underground were empty mines where salt deposits had been exhausted. These were now used for the eternal storage of nuclear waste from the production of atomic bombs.

As an engineer, I had access to every nook and cranny of this facility, including the mines. There were unsealed chambers intended for the storage of nuclear waste. These mines were air-conditioned, and hermetic gates were used to prevent even the smallest radioactive particles from reaching the earth's surface. The Department of Energy had spent hundreds of millions of dollars on this project but could not officially open it. The rooms were empty, although they had been prepared to contain nuclear waste. Several congressmen had stopped the opening of this facility under the banner of environmental protection.

The Department of Energy, which is a government agency, had tried to open this facility through a court order but had failed. This game has been going on for four years. The opening of this facility is a must, but the people's pressure on congressmen and the strong laws of democracy are fully felt in this case.

I stayed in a hotel with an indoor pool and Jacuzzi. All in all, it wasn't too bad; I was able to pay all my current bills. For some major holidays, I was flying home to California.

Ela came to my place on vacation, and she had an adventure on the way. Since she was traveling in the vicinity of the Mexican border, there were checkpoints on the road to check papers of permanent residence in the States. Border protection representatives ask whether you are an American citizen. If you are not, then they ask for a green card (i.e., a permanent visa). Ela, even though she was about to become an American citizen, did not have a green card with her. It took her two hours to convince the guards that she was not smuggling. Despite various controls, the Latino and Latina population has grown tremendously in the border states. Now even Florida, Texas, and California are complaining to the Federal Authorities that the influx of large numbers of undocumented noncitizens are causing enormous losses to the budgets of these states.

The loopholes in the legislation mean that undocumented noncitizens have access to all social rights, such as medical treatment, education, and various types of benefits. Yet these same residents in the States do the hardest jobs for little money and pay taxes. Immigration is very good for America, because immigrants work harder than Americans and are like fresh blood for this country. Democrats are now calling for open borders because immigrants are likely to vote for them in the future.

Ela arrived late in the evening, and we had a ceremonial welcome after two months of separation. The next day, it was Eli's birthday, so we celebrated it with an elegant dinner at the restaurant, and later with dancing in a local café. Little cowboys wore big hats and stepped on their shoes while dancing.

During the weekend, we went on a trip to some famous caves. Together with the guide and a small group, we first climbed and then went on a long underground walk. Huge caves, several hundred meters underground, stretched for about two kilometers. We admired dozens of mineral formations created by nature.

Until recently, the entrance to these caves were inhabited by thousands of bats. I think these little mammals moved away as the masses of visiting people started to pour in. Each of us had a flashlight or a lantern, because they were needed in the second part of the trip, which took us through undeveloped caves. A former military man allowed me to use his infrared binoculars, through which I could see in the dark. We returned to the hotel tired but happy. For a girl, Ela was doing very well on this thrilling trip.

The next day, we had a picnic by the river. It had once flowed on the surface, sometimes underground. This was an interesting phenomenon unknown to me up to that point. Three years later, Ela remembered this vacation as one of the best in her life.

I will leave the matter of subsequent contracts alone for the time being. Sometimes they were here; sometimes they were gone. Despite this, I always managed somehow. My real interest lay in politics and economics.

CHAPTER 4

IN THE ROLE OF A TOASTMASTER

★ ★ ★

I have always been interested in politics and liked to talk about politics. That is probably why, having a bit more free time, I joined the Toastmasters club, which is a speakers' club. I had no ambition to become Cicero or Cato; I just wanted to share my thoughts on the world, politics, and economics with people. In this chapter, I quote some of my more important speeches that I made in the club.

What Is Wrong?

I ask, What's wrong with America? Why are we in a recession now and Germany and Japan aren't? Our deficit is $300 billion a year. We borrow this amount every year to pay off our budget expenses. Isn't it better to limit these expenses? After all, loans with interest must be repaid by us, our children, our grandchildren—generations of Americans!

We are far too much a "welfare state." Let those who benefit from state care work for the minimum wage instead of constantly receiving aid, which plunges them into greater poverty.

Of the US budget, 40 percent is absorbed by the government. By comparison, in 1920, maintaining the government cost only 10 percent. So it is obvious that our administration is too extensive!

The USA is the richest country in the world, but for how long? Many economic and political powers have collapsed: Egypt, Greece, Rome. Also, former modern powers, such as Spain and Great Britain, are not playing in the premier league today. And this happened as a result of political mistakes and a lack of social discipline.

I can see some fundamental problems that will shape America's future. The number-one problem is education. This is generally weak in our country. We put a lot of money into it, but to no avail. When my son Roger was going to school, I asked the headmistress why homework was not being assigned. In response, I heard that this was due to the opposition of families. If it took the children more than twenty minutes to do their homework a day, there would be a protest.

Well, I remember another school in Europe. Here in the States, students do not respect teachers, and parents and teachers do not teach discipline, a sense of duty, and responsibility from childhood. Children use calculators and computers too much, so they don't exercise their minds with calculating. Watching TV and computer games have replaced book reading. Generally, schools do not have a high standard of education and upbringing.

There is also a politician's mistake. We educate too many lawyers and not enough scientists, engineers, and doctors. What, I ask, will be the economic condition of a country where the majority of educated citizens produce nothing but court cases?

Problem number two is the threat of crime. Here I can see the two main causative agents: drugs and the general availability of firearms. Managing this evil is not easy, but one must act consistently (i.e., make people, especially young people, aware of the tragic effects of using drugs, severely punish the production and trade of narcotic drugs, and introduce regulations that make it difficult to buy weapons).

Health care seems to be the number-three problem. We spend 14 percent of gross national income for this purpose, which is almost twice as much as Germany and Japan, and the standard of medical services in those countries is higher. The average American is more afraid of losing his or her medical insurance than his or her job, and some families spend $15,000 a year on it. Medical services are expensive, and a health crisis can cost a lifetime's savings.

Added to this is the demoralization of doctors! According to the *Los Angeles Times*, as many as 60 percent of operations are performed without medical need, just to allow surgeons to earn money. And a thing as obvious and justified as visitation to a patient's home is not practiced by American doctors. Why? Out of convenience! It's time to create a national social insurance fund!

And the fourth problem is economics. It is the last one on my list, but it is of the greatest importance. Americans no longer needs to be afraid of communism; now there is a different economic threat—from China, Japan, and the European community. During the Cold War, we spent $291 billion on armaments, neglecting research, production, and the economy. We should export more—especially cars and technical equipment.

Domestic production is neglected. After all, the VCR was invented in the United States, but we do not have a single factory producing video cameras! Not a single factory here produces fax machines! We no longer make our own large TV sets, and we import steel from abroad. There are many other such examples! American capital moves abroad, where work is cheaper, environmental regulations are lighter, and taxes are lower.

It is not true that California (the world's seventh largest economic power) is prone to recession. Not anymore! The number of arms contracts is declining, and the industry is moving out of California, where production costs and taxes are lower, work is more efficient, and water resources are richer.

It is up to the government to help the economy, first and foremost by establishing cheaper investment loans, eliminating unnecessary bureaucracy, and not collecting excessive demands from the unions. This will encourage industry to stay put.

The Japanese and the Chinese enter our market without any problems, but vice versa? Why

have American companies not entered the Far
East markets? Are Asians patriots who are more
willing than us to buy domestic products? Or
maybe their work is cheaper and more efficient.
Well, the US economy is losing ground inch by
inch, and the government is backing everyone except their citizens!

Americans themselves listened to me. I thought they might be
offended that some immigrant was criticizing their country. But
it was the opposite; I received a lot of applause, which meant that
my comments were right. Well, I'd lived half my life in the United
States, it was my second home country, and I knew its ills. And all
the evil started, in my opinion, back in the sixties, with liberalism,
the hippie movement, and so forth.

I am pleased to say that views similar to mine were made by
Ross Perot a few months later in a televised speech.

I wrote my speech in March 1992; in 1994, and President
Clinton, a Democrat, was trying to solve the problems I had
named. He intended to abolish welfare (i.e. benefits for the poor)
and replace them with training and job-creation programs. The
idea was right, but I was unsure whether it would succeed.

Welfare benefits were introduced under Nixon to reduce the
sphere of poverty, but the effect turned out to be the opposite; the
number of poor increased!

Another thing Clinton did was cut administration spending
and cut back on the large apparatus. But isn't that just about
gaining popularity? Among the highly industrialized countries,
the USA still has the weakest education, especially secondary and
primary education. There are hundreds of school districts, each
with its own curriculum. This does not work! There should be one
general national curriculum covering all schools. American children attend school approximately fifty days less than, for example,

Japanese children, as a result of free Saturdays, holidays, and so forth. I don't mention teachers' strikes anymore! Added to this is the demoralizing educational liberalism. A child who is not educated and is a hooligan must not be disciplined, for this child has the right to sue in court! The divorce of children from their parents is complete nonsense! Of course, this is another treat for attorneys.

There has been some progress in fighting crime. Some states, including California, already have laws that put the perpetrators of serious crimes in prison for life under conditions of triple recidivism. This is opposed by liberals. There are many voices against this law because they claim that it takes enormous sums to build prison buildings. Others in the ruling elite think that prisons do not need air-conditioning or television, and that a barracks would be enough. I support this point of view.

Regarding the restriction of access to weapons, a step was taken in the right direction when Congress passed a bill and the president signed it into law, banning the trade in machine guns. A hunters' union strongly protested this, as if hares were to be taken with heavy machine guns. I understand that the free possession of guns has been part of the American tradition from the very beginning, but even the most sacred tradition should be dictated by reason. Several thousand people die each year in America from gunfire!

The year 1994 is famous for an attempt at health care reform by Clinton and his administration. In short, Clinton proposed that every employee should have employer-paid insurance. The problem was that 40 million citizens did not have medical insurance, and the health-care system was costing the state $800 billion a year. In my opinion, it costs less to maintain hospitals where the poor can be treated, and the rich could have the choice of private visits. This is the case in Canada, for example. Americans, however, were afraid of introducing the Canadian system, in which the waiting time for surgery was fourteen days, while in the US it was only ten. These four days of difference were not, in my opinion, the main problem. The worst thing was that private insurance companies, acting as intermediaries, had grown richer through the ineffective system. Clinton's reform could have eliminated them and thus reduced the costs of medical services. However, the debates did not seem to go in that direction.

Economy
Over the past few weeks, economists have expressed their views to the Rostkowski Committee. I listened to their statements and discussions for hours. I was surprised that none mentioned that America needed to be more export oriented. Japan and Germany, countries that export a lot, are not in a recession like us, and their currencies are strong. And we have a negative trade balance with both Japan and Germany; Japan's negative balance is $41 billion a year. We also have negative balances with other Asian countries, though perhaps not to such an extent as this.

The competitive struggle for world markets has a long history. Today we are losing this fight, and we are doing nothing to turn the situation around. Right now, President Bush is visiting Asia with a group of industrialists. One of the goals of the visit is to talk with the Japanese about unfavorable trade. Such trade is disadvantageous, of course, for us, because our market is completely open and theirs are protected. The liberal experiment does not bear good fruit; we are losing to the allied economies of China, Germany, and Japan. It can be said that the Chinese, Germans, and the

Japanese teach us lessons in the business success that we must not ignore. But I don't believe in the success of Bush's visit to Japan. The Japanese prime minister is not voluntarily going to giving up these benefits. Yes, the Japanese promise something, but it ends with promises. Our government, our president—I think they should demand specific commitments, not promises.

In 1988, Canada signed a duty-free trade agreement with us. US exports rose immediately by $12.3 billion a year, and Canada has benefited greatly from this as well. You have to know that a billion-dollar increase in American exports results in twenty thousand new jobs for Americans!

In 1990, Mexican president Carlos Salinas de Gortari, an economist by profession, asked to sign a similar treaty with America. In 1991, Congress gave the Bush administration the so-called fast track for negotiations with Mexico. Once the agreement is signed, we will benefit, and the Mexican economy will significantly accelerate. On the other hand, as opponents argue, there may be an outflow of low-qualified work abroad that is not beneficial for the USA.

Forecasts for the European market look bleak for us. A future united Europe with duty-free trade and a common currency may turn out to be economically hermetic for America.

Under these conditions, we would need a European partner with a central location, a stable economy, and a political situation—a partner who would have traditionally friendly relations

with the USA. I think that Poland could become
a partner!

A possible duty-free trade agreement with
Poland would compensate the States for their
weak position in Europe and Asia, and hundreds
of thousands of highly qualified Polish engineers,
technicians, and workers could significantly raise
the standard of living. Poland should be strong in
the view of future Russian aggression.

Political Analysis
After my previous speeches, I was praised for their
content but criticized for the way they were delivered, As I was mainly reading from my notes and
not making eye contact with the audience.

Most politicians in Congress read from cards,
caring more about conveying the content than the
beauty of the speech. Even Churchill, considered
a great speaker, pretended that he did not need a
sheet of paper but looked at his notes through spe-
cially removed glasses. Of course, I agree that we,
the members of the club, are not politicians and
therefore should try to master the art of oration
perfectly. Anyway, public speaking has the characteristics of acting, and that is why Mr. Reagan
is such a good speaker, although he did not want
to speak in our club.

What does a good politician do? A good politician collects facts and information, with which
he formulates forecasts and programs for the future. I like Mr. Tsongas. He is honest, supports
business and economic development, and is also
a supporter of duty-free trade. Unfortunately, he

doesn't have a Hollywood look and belongs to the wrong party, and therefore won't be elected. Historically, Democrats are for spending money and Republicans are for business.

Can you imagine a family that spends more than it earns? Such a family would not last long, though America somehow does this, although we do not have the capital for modernization and investments.

I support the approach of other democratic candidates regarding the issue of national medical insurance, though I like the Republican candidate Pat Buchanan for his style. When he says, "Close some military bases at home and abroad and allocate money to domestic industry," my heart grows! But unfortunately Mr. Buchanan is an advocate of total isolation, and therefore the opponent of duty-free trade agreements, which are, after all, a factor in America's economic growth, and therefore its international power!

Bush is an advocate of duty-free trade, but he is facing a deficit of another $120 billion to finance the Gulf War. In addition, he is accused of lacking the characteristics of a true leader of the country, plans, and future vision.

My Ideal candidate is the one who will say that the most important thing is the economy! My Ideal candidate will say no to raising taxes and to a greater deficit, and will also be against the expenses marked by the law.

My ideal candidate, along with national medical insurance, gun control, and severe penalties for criminals—especially drug traffickers—will be in favor of controlling welfare payments and reducing the deficit.

Unfortunately, my friends, I am afraid that at the moment neither I nor all of America has the perfect candidate!

Political Analysis 2

In my last speech, I spoke about my ideal candidate. A few weeks later, after watching Ross Perot's television speech, I concluded that he was the most destined to be the president of the United States—the "third force" that will break the stalemate in Congress and turn our country away from its present bad path.

Because we are currently experiencing economic stagnation on a global scale, on a local scale, our Californian one, we have a recession and 9 percent unemployment. Between 1987 and 1992, more than seven hundred factories moved beyond the TAN limits or established subsidiaries outside of California. That means we've lost our seats, labor, and tax income.

It is time to reverse this trend, which is caused by taxes on new industrial investments. California ranks forty-ninth, ahead of Rhode Island, in terms of business facilitation. South Dakota comes first.

There is a Japanese word, "*kaizen*," which means "improvement." In my opinion, it is the key to the Japanese economic miracle. "Kaizen" refers to gradual, never-ending improvement: doing little things better, setting an ever-higher standard of the production process in changing market conditions, and doing so quickly.

If something stays the same, there is no progress. The role of management is to make the products better and cheaper, so it establishes the standard operating procedure (SOP) (i.e., laws, regulations, and guidance) for all major product operations. The worker standing at the machine starts by strictly following products, but after a while, he thinks about improvements in his life. Improvement projects are communicated through individual or collective suggestions. They arise in every production department, at every level, and are highly endorsed and rewarded by management. Yes, the philosophy of kaizen looks roughly more toward harmonious collective action and thinking than, as in America and Europe, toward individual inventiveness and creativity. Kaizen requires a different type of leadership based on personal experience and belief, and not necessarily on authority, position, or age. Management must collaborate well with workers, and when that collaboration is lacking, kaizen will not bear fruit.

Kaizen starts with recognizing the problem. Where there is a problem, there is a need for improvement. And you can wait for the effect for three to five years.

Maybe, friends, it is worth introducing the word "kaizen" into the language of our economy.

My War with the City
For the first time in one of my speeches I am touching on a personal matter, but I do so because it has a general agreement. It is not only about my conflict with the authorities of the Villa Park city

but also about all conflicts between private property and municipal interests in general.

On February 23, 1991, I applied for a permit to build a ten-foot wall with an electric gate around my house on South Loma Street. The bord rejected my application 2 to 3. And yet I had a good reason: the street noise was taking its toll on me more and more.

Two years later, there was a public meeting to donate my land to the city of Villa Park, and then I was able to speak to a local news reporter and make my case. And it was like that; after canceling and receiving the permit, I called the surveyors, and from their measurements I discovered that the city, given the plans to expand the street, was going to take away 330 feet of my property, which was half of my plot. I asked the city engineer why they had to move the street toward my house when they could use the lane on the other side, and I learned that the other side belonged to the city of Orange. Since my private wall-building project and their municipal street widening were in conflict, I was ordered to stop my project. And shortly thereafter, my building permit was revoked altogether. So I lost nearly $6,000, because that was the cost of my drawings, measurements, permits, and a lawyer.

But I took my way and offered the city about nine thousand square feet of my land (along with my construction materials to expand that damn street) as a donation—a donation worth approximately $180,000. It was this offer that caused the public meeting mentioned above to be called on January 26, 1993.

Now listen: the city refused my generous offer! But in the rejection, their attorney publicly stated that this land belongs to me. Before that, he had said it belongs to the city. So I have them in the palm of my hand. If they want to widen the street, they have to come to me and buy this land from me. The fifth *Human Rights Appendix to the United States Constitution* clearly states that "private property cannot be taken without a fair payment." In June 1996, the matter was still unsettled. The city still wanted land from me and would probably have paid by now. But the attorney I hired for the case sent a letter to the city council demanding that they pay $327,000 for this piece of land and my troubles with it. Sometimes it is worth getting a Jewish attorney; they can be unscrupulous.

The future will show how this matter will be handled.

Invest in Real Estate
California real estate value is going up and down. Graphically it is like a sine wave, and we are currently at the bottom point (i.e., in recession.

We're going to be talking about money, so I'm going to use summary formulas.

V (value) = I (annual income): R (percentage of return).

For example, if a building's net value is $1,000,000, $100,000 is a net income of 0.10, so the return is 10 percent. We have four types of profit tests, and here is an example: the purchase price of a building is $85,000. Now, in California, prices are two to three times higher, but these numbers are just an example. The loan is $65,000. This is the magic of "leverage"—you buy using money that is not yours. The difference is your investment, which is $20,000.

Test 1—return on investment: Let's assume that the annual net income is $10,000 and the annual loan fee (debt return and interest) is $9,000. The difference between these sums is the so-called liquid cash. In this case, $1,000 in liquid cash and $20,000 of your investment means there is a 5 percent return on investment.

Test 2—debt reduction: With $2,000 of annual debt reduction and $20,000 as your investment, the return on annual debt reduction is 0.10, or 10 percent.

Test 3—savings in paying taxes through depreciation (consumption of fixed assets): Buildings, which are subject to wear, account for 80 percent of the purchase price. The price of the land is 20 percent, and the land is not consumed. $85,000 × 0.80 = $68,000. This is the portion for the purchase of the building. The economic "life" of a building is twenty years. 100 percent divided by twenty years shows that this consumption occurs at a rate of 5 percent per year. That is, $68,000 × 0.05 (5%) = $3,400. This is the annual amount allowed for consumption. Suppose you are in the 50 percent tax bracket. (Luckily there are no such high taxes anymore; now the highest is 44 percent, the average is 28 percent, and the lowest is 15 percent). In this case, $3,400 × 0.5 (50%) = $1,700, which is your additional income (as no taxes are paid on consumption). Your return on consumption is $700.

Test 4—increment factor: Suppose your neighborhood shows a 5 percent increase in the value of its real estate on average during the year. This is not an exorbitant example, because there was a time in California that the increase was 30 percent. Over the year, the increase in value is $85,000 (purchase price) × 0.05 (5%) (property value increment) = $4,250. The percentage of value increase is 21.25 percent, based on your purchase price of $20,000.

When we add up all the percentages of returns from the four tests, we get 44.75 percent, and as we can see, the investment shows quite a good return. A real estate agent will not teach you this, because he is not in business to make you money. There are two main problems with real estate: getting a loan and keeping it.

When buying a property, you must qualify for a loan of 80 to 90 percent of the purchase price with all documents and 75 percent of the partial documentary. Also remember that real estate is quite difficult to sell, so think about whether you can afford to maintain it.

Are We a Falling Democracy?

Many wise people in our beloved country try to answer some simple questions, such as the following:

- Why is our economy tipping downwards?
- Why is there such chaos in our society?

We are great international policemen. We know how to temper the irresponsible behavior of other nations, but we do not know how to recognize our internal problems.

Mr. Newt Gingrich, the chairman of the US Congress, in his book *To Renew America* said, "America is the leading country on our planet, with the largest economy in the world, and it provides opportunities and happiness to all kinds of people, from different cultures, more than any country in the history of the world." On the other hand, our civilization is on the verge of collapse, with the poor and criminals in the pits of our social classes and in the centers of our cities, and with an economy heavily pressed by the rival economies of Germany, Japan, and China.

Intellectual liberal nonsense, such as unlimited freedom of choice and the freedom to perform irresponsible acts, was propagated in the 1960s by the mass media, universities, and some religious and political leaders. Currently, as a result of these views, our family values do not exist, the ability to teach the young generation is crippled, and our young generation is lost. Some say that in a hundred years America will not exist if something is not done about it.

We will have fewer and fewer scientific and technological inventions. Our economy will lag behind those of our competitors more and more. No civilization can survive when twelve-year-olds have children, fifteen-year-olds kill each other, eighteen-year-olds die of AIDS, and eighteen-year-olds get diplomas even though they can't read.

According to a report released by the Department of Education, 50 percent of US residents cannot read English. Teachers no longer teach spelling and do not use a red pencil for corrections to keep children under emotional stress.

Only the parents who raise their children are responsible for the children's attitudes and outlooks on life. When a child goes to school, his character is already formed. Some accuse the media (movies, books, press, music) of irresponsible behavior. The media are also the parents. Let's stop wondering who is responsible for what and keep shifting the blame onto something or someone. You have to start setting a good example yourself.

For example, we allowed a twelve year old girl to appear with her mother on a television show and her mother to say in front of millions of TV viewers that she allowed her daughter to have sexual relations with her boyfriend at home so that she would not get into more trouble.

In addition to the existing nonsensical sex education in schools, some groups are pushing for homosexual education in primary schools. Distributing condoms for free in high schools and universities is stupid because students should be focused on academic and sports achievements. I raised my two sons in this country, and it was not an easy task. Young people in our country have one thing in mind: having fun, having fun, and having fun again.

We are not the first civilization to rot from within. But we are the first generation in American history to face these kinds of problems. By definition, civilization is based on the previous generation. There is no doubt that our postwar generation has completely collapsed it.

Each generation is faced with a series of serious tasks, and showing passivity can mean the end of our civilization in an extremely short time.

General De Gaulle once said, "A nation can be devastating itself through inappropriate policies and moral decay. Poor leadership and failure to respond to existing problems lead to a violent national collapse." If people murder or rape, it is not their fault; it is the fault of society. If a teenager becomes pregnant, it is not her, her boyfriend's, or her parents' fault; it is the fault of society. If the children do not want to study, it is not the fault of the education system; it is the fault of society.

According to this widely repeated stupid theory, society has such enormous power that it is responsible for everything that no one is personally responsible for anything.

America has never been a land of saints. But we gradually destroy ourselves by accepting the current situation. We must stop rape and violence.

Recently, in Los Angeles, a three-year-old girl lost her life to a bullet when her parents' car accidentally turned onto a street where a gang was prowling. A twelve-year-old boy lost his life on the highway to bullets fired from a speeding car.

If children don't get lessons from their parents or the educational system, then where are they to learn from? What can we do to make the nation stop this vicious circle? At the heart of our national problem are children and education. My initial questions can be addressed as follows:

High-level school programs for each school in the US should be sourced centrally from the Department of Education. As of now, each school district has its own program, which does not promise success. The educational status in our country should be given highest priority. Children must be taught to be personally responsible and to respect parents, teachers, and authorities. The only institution that can implement such a policy is the administration of a strong president. Of the candidates for the presidency in the 1996 election, not a single one would talk about such problems. Education and election is a national security matter and should be control by a division of the federal government, such as the US Department of Defense.

Racism is a huge problem in our society. We have written rights that should be respected: all are equal and have equal starts and career rights. That should be the end of the discussion. The media should stop discussing this problem and dividing our society. Everyone, black or white, has prejudices, and it's impossible to completely change human nature.

From the court cases of Councilor King, the Menendez brothers, and O. J. Simpson, it can be seen that the legal system in our racially divided society is failing. This system worked well in white England, but it does not work in colorful America. In my opinion, a professional jury is a pretty good idea.

If we can solve the problems I wrote about, then we will have a heaven on earth in our beloved America.

CHAPTER 5

A FEW REMARKS ON THE CAPITALIST ECONOMY

★ ★ ★

I am not an economist by profession, but an engineer who, working in business, has learned economics from the practical side. Therefore, I have no ambition to elaborate on academic arguments; I only want to help the reader, especially the Polish reader, understand how the so-called capitalist system works.

In any economic system, four elements determine production. In the case of capitalism perfected by governmental control, these elements are land, labor, capital, and the free initiative of an energetic and inventive individual. It is easy to notice that in the absence of at least one of these elements, no economic operation will be possible.

If we want a normal capitalist economy in Poland, we must first regulate land ownership. This is because no investor, especially a foreign one, will decide to build a factory in an area that will not be its property or at least a perpetual lease. If in Poland, in the vast majority of cases, it is not clear who the land belongs to, then the investor simply does not know from whom to buy or lease the land and whether the person or institution with whom he wants to conclude the contract is entitled to do so.

It is no coincidence that Chancellor Kohl, seeking loans in the US for the development of former East Germany, insisted that in East Germany property rights to land are already settled!

Two-thirds of American wealth is real estate, mostly concentrated in cities, where 80 to 90 percent of the population lives. American democracy is reflected in the free economy, in which real estate plays a very significant role. There are five types of real estate, namely residential houses, commercial buildings, industrial facilities, farms, and special-purpose buildings. Residential houses occupy, on average, half of the city area. In the economic sense, they form two markets: buying/selling and renting. Commercial buildings are those which constitute the basis for trade and services (i.e., shops, office buildings).

On average, they do not occupy about 15 percent of the area of cities. The industry covers 5 to 10 percent of the area of cities, and we divide it into light and heavy. It has a fundamental impact on the development of the agglomeration, as it provides jobs and taxes.

Hence, local authorities often establish fiscal breaks to attract industry. Farms provide food (strictly raw material for food production), wood, flowers, and so on. On the other hand, special-purpose buildings are theaters, churches, parks, and historical buildings, which together usually occupy about 1 percent of the city's area.

In America, each of these types of real estate must be grouped in a properly designated area by the authorities (i.e., the law of the relevant zones, called "zoning," must be respected). In Poland, there are probably no such regulations, or at least they are not respected, since residential buildings can stand near factories; in the United States, this would be unacceptable, for ecological reasons!

One of the main reasons for immigrating to America was the desire to have land and a home. Absolute respect for private property at relatively low prices was a magnet that attracted people from all over the world to the United States. Private ownership of real estate brings benefits not only in the economic dimension but also psychologically, ensuring a sense of stability and security. The experience of peoples and societies clearly shows that without the right to freely own property and the freedom to sell, there is no free economy, and probably no real economy at all!

The real estate market affects all other markets. However, a relatively small percentage of people buy there for cash; most try to qualify for bank loans. As a curiosity, I would like to add that Muslims are forced to buy for cash because their religion forbids taking out loans and paying interest.

Economics is the science of wealth, which is what society produces, transmits, and consumes. I remember that in the second year of the polytechnic, I studied the political economy of capitalism in the first semester. Somehow it was easy for me to understand what profit was and what the costs were, and I got a B on my final exam. The next semester was the economics of socialism, in which I got only a C. I am strangely reluctant to think of this model of the economy based on state subsidies.

In addition to the so-called pure economics taken straight from academic textbooks, we have a practical "applied" economy that works across the board.

Two economic theories are known: positive and relief. The first analyzes the elements of the market and focuses solely on economic aspects; the second connects ethical and social goals to the economy.

Economists like to imitate the accuracy of mathematicians and often use formulas to describe phenomena. In real economic life, however, there are so many variables that not everything can be reduced to a theoretical, mathematical pattern. Nevertheless, many basic economic laws work plainly in reality, such as the law of supply and demand. A fairly strict regularity also occurs in the mutual generation of phenomena. For example, reducing inflation causes unemployment to rise, and the endless attempts by governments around the world to find a middle ground tend to fail.

An important economic concept is an increment. An increment is an increase in the national production potential as far as possible. The gain is sometimes difficult to measure. For example, since the beginning of the century, the American laborer has gained thirty hours of free time per week, which is a large profit, though it is not included in gross national income. Economic growth in the USA is about 3 percent, and in Japan it is about 8 percent. Such comparisons are difficult because of different definitions of national income and different accounting methods.

There are three economic indicators: leading, resultant, and lagging. Leading indicators generally predict what will happen to the economy in general in the future. Unemployment and indebtedness are resultant indicators of the condition of the economy at a given moment. Investments, or the level of public credit, are lagging indicators, as they lag behind an increase or a decline in business activity.

Now for a magic term that we would like to be as far away from as possible: "economic planning." Yes, that's the famous communist planning. The capitalist economy is mixed, and apart from the market, there are also elements of state planning and intervention making up the so-called economic policy. Here are some examples: with high unemployment, the government—if, of course, it has the resources—can order public works; when purchasing power declines, the government can cut taxes; when investment shrinks, the government may reduce the interest rates on investment loans.

There was once a French industrialist named Legendre who,

when asked what the government could do for the industry, replied, "laissez nous faire."

This means "leave us alone." These words were the basis for the term "laissez-faire," meaning the total non-interference of government in the economy.

In the late seventeenth and early eighteenth centuries, monarchs heavily interfered with the economies of France and England. The doctrine of a truly free liberal economy comes from the eighteenth-century economist Adam Smith and was effective (in an economic sense) during the period of the formation of capitalism. Today's liberals, headed by Milton Friedman, regard Smith as their spiritual father.

In the following period, as a result of social conflicts and economic crises (especially the Great Depression of the 1930s), the economic role of the state grew and the concept of interventionism was born, created mainly by Keynes. Elements of Keynesianism are still firmly embedded in the American economy today.

Free economic activity is characterized by private ownership and initiative. It is a capitalist concept that has passed its historical test everywhere. Speaking of private property, we see once again the important role that real estate plays. Private activity results in private activity—that is, production, trade, and services. In practice, this free activity consists of the fact that the entrepreneur employs whomever he wants (in America with equal rights, regarding things such as race), produces what he wants and what he wants (this is prompted by the market), and sets prices corresponding to the market. Society benefits from the jobs created by the entrepreneur and the taxes paid by him.

Capital is an important factor. It can be material (machines, buildings, land) or immaterial (the company's tradition, logo, patents, buildings and their land, and other necessary things). The capital invested is the sum of the net worth of the corporation plus long-term loans.

When corporate directors approve of certain sums for new factories or new equipment, it is called "capital expenditure." Capital expenditure is a very important figure in a country's economy. If it is low, economic growth is generally low. In the seventies, capital expenditure was only 7 percent of the national budget (GNP) (i.e., 3 percent less than in the previous period).

Profit, of course, is the selling price minus the buying costs. This is a form of earnings, as opposed to percentages or normal income.

By "intensive industrial capital" we mean the enormous sums needed for an operation as compared to the number of workers required for these operations or the amount of final production. For example, such a ratio is high; in furniture production, it is low; and in highly developed countries, intensive capital prevails.

"Market capital" deals with long-term investments and savings. These include long-term government promissory notes as well as universal stocks. These are investments considered risk-free and easy to sell.

Money is a fun topic of conversation. Money is a unit of value, and almost anything can be expressed in money, be it in zlote or dollars. In advanced economies, money is used for settlement and exchange, but it cannot be relied on with great accuracy for the simple reason that its value fluctuates. We work hard for it, save it, and often forget that it has no intrinsic value, but only symbolic value. The invention of money is a wonderful achievement of the human imagination. In primitive or pathological Oak economies (e.g., in camps, prisons, or some socialist countries), the equivalent of money is some good: shells, tobacco, or vodka, for example.

The first money was made of precious metals. Gold, silver, and copper were ideally suited as means of payment because of their relatively difficult accessibility, high durability, easy recognition, constant value, and divisibility. For example, the word "ruble" comes from the fact that this coin could be chopped with an ax into two or four parts.

In the middle of the eighteenth century, a goldsmith from London founded the first bank. People gave him gold for safe-keeping and received receipts in return. This was the beginning of paper money. In the same century, the practice of issuing authorizations was established based on which other people could take the deposited gold from the goldsmith. This, in turn, started the checking system.

After some time, the goldsmith realized that not all of the depositors were receiving their gold, and the stock was growing. So he started to lend these reserves at a high interest rate, launching a modern banking system. To this day, banks, although they are obliged to pay out deposited sums on demand, lend more than they have in their accounts. It took a long time for banks to become quite safe.

In Russia, paper money was introduced by Catherine the Great, but it was covered not in gold, but the ground.

What is so special about gold that everyone has treasured it for thousands of years? Firstly, it is a metal that cannot be produced, and secondly, it is indelible. Gold can protect a spacecraft from radiation, and a seal made of gold lasts a lifetime. About 65 percent of gold is used by jewelers, about 5 percent by dentists, 5 percent by the electronics industry, and 12 percent by mints. Still, about 3 percent goes to medals and medallions, and the other 6 percent remains in speculative and investment transactions.

All the gold that has been extracted over thousands of years amounts to about one hundred thousand tons, and it is still circulating the world in various roles and forms. Dollars are no longer backed by gold, and the same is true of most currencies. Gold has two prices in America: the official price ($35 per ounce) set by the so-called Bretton Woods Agreement to stabilize the dollar in the price of gold, and the normal, speculative market price, which today is about $460 an ounce. The world's largest gold deposit, nearly 40% of the world's gold resources, is held by the Federal Reserve Bank at Ft. Knox, Kentucky.

The Federal Reserve Bank, also known simply as the Fed, oversees enormous exchanges, precisely in gold, involving states, corporations, and individual billers. When Germany demanded the return of borrowed amounts in gold, the problem of costly and safe transportation across the Atlantic arose. So bookkeeping was used, and the gold was simply transferred to a special "German Room" at the Fed.

Apart from the transactions made by the Fed, gold is generally not in circulation. There are two basic means of payment in America: dollars and checks. We are waiting for the holders of checking accounts at commercial banks to pay. A given citizen pays a certain amount to the bank, which the bank has the right to charge for operation, and he can pay with checks as and when he wants until the account is exhausted. Economists term the total of all cash in banknotes, coins, and checking accounts as M-1. Checking accounts account for around 75 percent of M1. There are also higher categories—M-2, M-3, M-4, M-5, M-6, M-7—depending on understandable assumptions. Every Thursday afternoon, the Fed releases a report on the exact size of the M-1. The report appears in the Friday issues of the *Wall Street Journal* and the *New York Times*. It is important to know the value of M-1, as it influences the leading indicator (i.e., it allows one to predict the economic situation in the near future).

I will now touch upon an interesting topic, which is how money is created in the United States. Of course, this is not just, as many people think, a matter of printing banknotes and minting coins. The money-making process is controlled by the Federal Reserve Board (FRB) and the Federal Open Market Committee (FOMC). Broadly speaking, the Federal Reserve System is run by

FRB and FOMC. This targeting is done in several ways. Banks that also belong to the system are an important factor. These banks must hold an appropriate amount of cash, which is called "reserves." By establishing a higher reserve, the Fed limits the amount of cash that banks can offer in the form of loans.

Reducing the reserve, of course, is the opposite and is economically creative, as loans create investment and jobs. Loans are very important to the economy; thanks to them, there is a so-called multiplying effect. It works as follows: a bank borrows money that is deposited into another bank's account. The interbank transfer is made by telephone bookkeeping. Physically, money does not travel from bank to bank. The second way is that the client himself takes money from one bank and deposits it into the other. So if someone gets a loan, the money travels from bank to bank. Interestingly, there is a multiplying effect when it comes to borrowing money. This money goes to other banks, which get more reserves and thus have more money to lend.

The Fed dictates the amount of the reserve offered to banks. This is called fractional reserve banking. It is needed in case you need to withdraw cash from your accounts at a specific time. Most banks hold a reserve that they have to be able to pay out within one day. Such a system allows bankers to borrow more cash than they have on hand—assuming, of course, that all people do not turn up to banks on the same day to request withdrawals from their accounts. To reassure bank customers that their savings are safe, The federal government created the Federal Deposit Insurance Corporation (FDIC), the government's bank account insurance for up to $100,000, which keeps people from panicking.

I will now demonstrate an example of how this system works. Suppose you have $1,000 in your account and the government has instructed the bank to keep only 20 percent on hand as a reserve, which is $200 for your account. The remaining $800 is borrowed at interest. The loaned $800 goes to another bank, which also obliged to keep 20 percent and can loan 80 percent, which is $640. The borrowed $640 will go to the next bank, and again the 20 percent reserve will fall off and $512 will remain. When five banks are involved in the process, the sum of the borrowed money will be $2,668, while the savings and checking accounts will be $3,361. If we add reserves to money borrowed by banks and to savings and checking accounts, we get a total of $6,721. This is how much money was created by the initial payment of your $1,000! The fewer reserves banks have to keep on hand, the more they can borrow and thus stimulate spending and investment.

Let's see if there are any bugs in this system. If people hide their savings in their socks instead of at the bank, the system will not work. Also, the presence of too much money in the market is a risk, as it causes inflation. Inflation is a disease of the economy; it destroys markets, although the real estate market, for example, is defending itself quite effectively. The more money on the market, the lower the percentage on loans, and thus the greater availability of credit.

Demand is growing, taking precedence over supply, which leads to higher prices. This is inflation. For some, it is misfortune; for others, pure profit. Of course, inflation is a drama for people who live on a salary. For the government, inflation is beneficial because increased wages mean higher taxes, so you can say that inflation is an additional, hidden, tax. Banks that lend money will be affected by inflation, because they will not actually make back the value of their debts, and additionally, as a result of the increase in interest rates, the number of people eligible for loans will decrease. To prevent inflation, the bank's reserve must be controlled. The point is not to "loosen" banks excessively by letting money into the market. The monetary policy conducted by the Fed is independent, free from the pressure of the administration or Congress.

The operation of the free market allows that the Fed or ordinary citizens can sell and buy stocks. When the Fed wants to increase the flow of money to the market, it buys stocks from citizens. Then people have more money and put it in banks. Banks can then borrow more, and borrowing, as we know, is the driving force behind the creation of new money. Conversely, when the Fed wants to curb the flow of money, it sells stocks.

The discount rate is the percentage the Fed charges to the banks it lends to. It is also another tool used to regulate the impact of money. If you want to borrow from a commercial bank, that bank must borrow from the Fed and pay the discount rate. If the Fed reduces the discount rate, it will encourage commercial banks to borrow, and thus, according to the mechanism already described, the amount of money in the market will increase.

Action, on the contrary (e.g., increasing the discount rate) works on loans to inhibit what.

We currently have a high discount rate, which is a result of the anti-inflationary policy of the Fed. This is the bottom of the economic cycle sine wave. To get out of it, one has to use the methods described above to increase the flow of money and stimulate demand and investments. The real estate market is the first to feel the recovery from recession and is therefore called a leading indicator. Conversely, with the rest of the economy at the height of a sinusoidal hump, the real estate market first enters recession for lack of credit or money to borrow.

The money should (1) be easily transferable (e.g. from one continent to another), (2) have a relatively constant value, and (3) be permanent.

Experience shows that in a crisis, when money loses its value, the demand for gold, coins, works of art, and other high-value tangible items increases.

Government intervention in the economy was a response to troublesome social problems caused by so-called pure capitalism.

These were (and still are) unemployment, the "unfair" distribution of the wealth produced, unfair business practices, poverty, economic instability, and economic stagnation.

The government tried to remedy all of this through

- job creation and unemployment insurance,
- protection of customers and employees,
- payment of unemployment benefits (welfare),
- artificial stabilizing action, and
- artificial strengthening of the economy through monetary policy.

People earn money in a variety of ways. The owner of an apartment house lives on rent, the clerk gets a salary, the banker gets the interest, and the businessman lives on the profit the company brings him. Most of this income is spent on goods and services. There are two primary markets: the source market and the product market. In the source market, buyers are businessmen and sellers are individuals—owners of land or capital, or workers selling their work. In the product market, buyers are individual customers and sellers are businesses offering products, goods, and services using land, labor, and capital previously acquired on the market.

The government is at the heart of these operations and levies a tax on every transaction in both markets. It then finances, by way of tax administration (millions of jobs), the armed forces, education and road construction, and some money simply goes back to the citizens (some) in the form of benefits and allowances. So wealth circulates from businesses to individuals (source market) and from individuals to businesses (product market) and from both to government in the form of taxes, and from there back to business and individuals in the form of government programs.

For a market to exist, five basic elements are needed:

- buyers and sellers
- purchasing power
- exchange
- items with value
- price negotiation

To say it all in one sentence, the market is where buyers and sellers meet to exchange items when negotiating prices. Every farmer who goes to the market square with cabbages or potatoes knows about this, but the Polish red government did not know it.

Procurement is the totality of goods that sellers offer at a specific price within a specified period. Demand is the totality of goods that buyers want to buy at certain times and prices. There is also a term, "effective demand," which refers to the willingness to buy goods at a certain time for a certain price, taking into account current opportunities. More credit stimulates demand; less credit lowers it.

Advertising strengthens demand, and fashion shapes customer preferences. Supply also has its own rules. When prices rise, producers offer more goods for sale, and only when they become cheaper is this trend reversed.

Supply and demand fluctuate, but in a normal market, there will always be an equilibrium point. Since the market is not always perfect, citizens demand that the government control it. One of the worst phenomena on the market, and generally one of the greatest misstatements of capitalism, is a monopoly.

A monopoly is a market having only one seller. An oligopoly is a market in which there are only a few sellers for the mass of buyers. A monopsony is a market in which there is only one buyer. These market issues make sources and profits unevenly distributed. The government tries to prevent one group from dominating the market and demands competition everywhere.

There are several factors taken into account when assessing the economic situation:

- gross national income
- the number of employed and unemployed
- per capita income and the number of inhabitants in the country

An economy is like a balloon that expands and contracts according to the amount of air pumped into it. It can also be represented graphically as a sine wave, with the humps representing booms and the troughs representing recessions. When a recession lasts too long, it turns into a depression. The first depression in America occurred in 1897 and lasted more than twenty years.

From 1897 to 1930, the Dow Jones Industrial Average increased by 1,800%. This average expresses in points the achievement of the five hundred largest American corporations, and currently the figure is over 5,000 points. The construction of railroads in the last century played a significant role in the development of the American economy. But already in 1907, production factors, such as land, labor, and capital, began to be very expensive, and as a consequence, there was a severe recession, which fortunately did not turn into a depression, as the market was not saturated yet and there was no overproduction.

In the nineteenth century, the railway contributed to the development in the twentieth century of the strengthening of the American economy. Many industries have since developed: fuel, rubber, metal. Roads and highways were built at a rapid pace. In 1913, Americans thought they had found a way to protect themselves from depression. It was this year that the Fed began operating.

The war in 1917 additionally boosted the pace of economic development. With the advent of jazz, stocks skyrocketed.

Westinghouse stock went from $92 to $313, RCA from $95 to $505, and the Dow Jones rose from 191 to 381 points. This miracle took place from 1927 to 1929, and then came the famous depression of the 1930s, which swept across the entire world. In addition to unemployment and poverty, the specter of communism hangs over America. It is terrifying to think what would have happened if the Communists, taking advantage of the crisis, had seized power.

Only war puts an end to depression. But the Republicans who had ruled America for seventy years had to give way to the Democrats. They owed Roosevelt a New Deal, a victory in the war, and the Yalta agreements with Russia. God and history will judge him.

After the war, the economy fluctuated between growth and recession, but the depression was no more. Of course, even today, we cannot with certainty predict whether a crisis like that of the 1930s will happen again someday, but in general, people are now more cautious and read economic indicators better.

After this short historical overview, let's come back to the basic concepts, indicators, and figures that will help you understand the health of the economy. Gross national product (GNP) is the sum of all expenditures on current products and services or the sum of all income from production and services.

In America, the value of production (and services) sold and unsold is expressed in dollars. Of course, this is calculated at current prices. The US GNP is $1 trillion dollars (and in 1975 was already $1.5 trillion), which is a thirteen-digit number.

Two-thirds of the US GNP is spent by the population on goods and services, 10 percent is used for government investment, and 25 percent is spent on the armed forces, highways, and state government spending. A separate component of GNP is export–import— or, more precisely, balance of trade (i.e., the difference between export and import).

If we take inflation into account when calculating GNP, we

get a lower sum referred to as "real GNP." The ratio of GNP to true GNP is called the "GDP deflator ratio," which is analogous to the so-called consumer price index—a useful tool for measuring inflation. The Bureau of Labor Statistics publishes monthly data on the consumer price index, and the Department of Commerce reports the current per capita income, which is the income per person after all taxes.

An important factor is employee productivity. It is shaped by many elements, including cooperation with management, level of motivation, and quality of tools. The hourly productivity of a private-sector employee in 1967 was assumed to be 100 percent. Currently, this productivity has increased by 20 percent.

Let's talk for a moment about the factors that allow us to fore-cast the development of the economy. These are the coefficients of the so-called pre-emptive. Sometimes they are downright funny. For example, it was noticed that the deterioration foreshadows the increased breeding of goats. This relationship seems inexplicable, but it is confirmed statistically. Maybe people, sensing bad times, want to save on milk? Another such interesting factor is the number of job losses. An increase in job losses is a sign of good economic conditions. When there is economic growth, people are less concerned with keeping their jobs.

Traditionally, the stock market is a valuable leading indicator. The *Business Conditions Digest*, with the help of the US Department of Commerce, issues a monthly economic forecast report. It includes charts and points to changes in economic activity.

The *Business Conditions Digest* uses the Standard and Poor's 500, which is an index of stock quotations of five hundred leading corporations launching shares on the market. Currently, this index is over 5,000 points. Its reliability does not raise any objections. It is obvious that when citizens have confidence in the economy, they buy shares. This indicator is also very valuable because it can be seen from day to day, and even from minute to minute.

It is up to the Fed to provide the money to the market. We know that money is fuel for the economy. When the market collapsed in 1929, no one was yet calculating the amount of cash delivered. If such calculations existed, it would have been concluded that money was scarce, and the catastrophe could have been prevented.

There are a total of twelve published leading indicators. They should not be taken for granted, but used as data for your business thoughts.

The problems most bothering the American economy include the following:

- national debt
- Medicare, or health care for the poor
- negative trade balance with many countries
- subsidies for agriculture
- unemployment
- help for abroad
- poverty and homelessness
- strikes

In 1986, a fiscal reform was carried out. The system was simplified, but it was not without errors. I believe that the elimination of tax reliefs and deductions for people who build houses is hampering the construction industry. At this time, one can deduct only the interest repaid for the loan taken out of the tax.

Until the Vietnam War, America was the world's largest lender. Today it is the most indebted country in the world. Why? Economists provide neither unequivocal answers nor miraculous solutions. They only provide tools for analysis. The rest is in the hands and heads of government and business. Besides, economics is the science of how society produces and distributes goods.

However, the universal goals that a free capitalist economy should pursue are as follows:

- price stabilization
- high income
- high investment income
- free trade between nations
- close economic cooperation among friendly nations
- sparing use of natural resources
- freedom from government restrictions
- protection for own producers
- increase in free time for employees
- stability of earnings and employment
- technological progress
- cooperation between economic groups
- increased competition
- government support for certain groups and industries

For the economy to be transparent, it is necessary to talk about it using a language that is understandable and balanced. When thinking about it, do not forget about common sense. Use understandable, simple tools when examining it.

CHAPTER 6

TRAVEL
EXPERIENCES

★ ★ ★

During all the years that I spent in America, day after day,
fighting a hard struggle for existence and, as a result,
breaking through from the immigrant lowlands to the
middle class, I have not forgotten my homeland for a moment.
Not only do I participate in Polish diaspora organizations, but I
also tried to help my compatriots both in the United States and
in the country. But above all, from the moment when the political situation allowed it, I started to visit Poland regularly. I knew
that the Polish economy, which was recovering from ideological
enslavement, needed my money and, especially, my experience
in business. And vice versa, as a businessman, I needed a young,
absorptive market (at that time it seemed to me that this market
was like that), in which I expected to do good business.

After twelve years in America, I finally went back to Poland. It
was 1986, so there had not yet been a political thaw, but there was
not a complete frost either. The proof that something was changing was showed in the very fact that I was granted a visa. In the
past, I had been regularly refused, systematically suggesting that

I renounce Polish citizenship. This time I had a strong argument in that as a donor to the children's hospital in Łomianki, I should meet its director. But let's not forget that even the most obvious arguments do not have to convince the Communists, and if they do, it means that the situation is changing for the better.

My first stay in the country after so many years, and especially my contact with my family, had something of the stereotypical "Uncle came from America" feel to it. This is a warning for Poles that they can alienate a guy like me who comes with dollars and with goodwill.

It started when they liked me having a car at my disposal, trips around the country, and banquets (at my expense), and it ended ... eh, better not to say.

An old saying goes, "The best way to go with your family is in the picture." Anyway, I had received signals earlier that the attitude of my Polish family toward me was not necessarily friendly. Well, when "Uncle from America" arrived, they expected money and invitations; when he did not pull them out of a hat like a magician, they started murmuring that Uncle was not good. I proposed to a relative who had butchering skills that we set up a sausage business together, and he willingly agreed. I bought sausage machines, and he was supposed to contribute his job and qualifications, but he withdrew at the last moment without warning. How stupid I was with the machines and the rented premises. Of course, in the end I sold it for a profit, but the disgust remained.

Such events create a bad atmosphere, and on top of that, everything that is poured out is the sauce of envy—the envy of a man who had done well in the States. I will come back to this topic.

I come from a merchant family, so what was I supposed to do in Poland if not trade? I realized that there was an absorptive market there for fashionable and cheap clothing, as well as electronics, toys, and gadgets. To make a profit in that market, one had to buy goods from the cheapest producers, and that's why I set off on a tour of the Far East. Apart from business, it was also an extremely interesting experience.

I'll start with Singapore. Americans had recently associated this country with a flogging penalty that was imposed on an American student for smearing cars with paint. Because of this, there was a lot of hype in the press (especially the left-wing press, of course), and even President Clinton himself joined in, appealing to reduce the number of clubs from six to four. I consider this kind of involvement of the president not serious. I am closer to the view of most citizens (according to polls) that the hooligan was fully entitled to having his ass beaten. Who knows whether it is worth considering introducing similar penalties in the USA. Because of vandalism, American cities do not look their best and are in a deplorable state. This solution is supported by the fact that crime rates in Singapore are many times lower than in the States.

I rate Singapore Airlines highly. It was a pleasant flight with good service. I flew from Frankfurt with a stopover in Bangkok, Thailand. The airport in Singapore is modern and nice, and as at any airport in the civilized world, you can book a hotel room there. Hotel prices fluctuated from $80 to $200; I chose a lower-range offer for $100. In the evening, I went out to the balcony of my room to look at the skyline and the city bustling with life; it was a city, or rather a state, that over fifty years ago was artificially separated by the British from Malaysia.

The founder of Singapore's economic success is widely believed to be Prime Minister Lee Kuan Yew, of Chinese origin but educated in the UK as a faculty of law. The local population is 70 percent Chinese and are hardworking, calm, and disciplined. Poland immediately came to mind. What future would it prepare for itself, and would it be able to find the right leader?

At night, a few leaflets advertising oriental massages were thrown at the door of the room, but I was not curious to check what they were all about.

The next day, after breakfast in a nice hotel restaurant, I went on foot to explore the city. I noticed that everything was clean and tidy. After lunch, I had a business meeting. An electronics company distributor offered me a container of large TVs at $400 apiece for delivery to Hamburg.

There were many nice places in the city where one could eat cheaply. Alcohol was quite expensive there. In an open street restaurant, all the tables were full, and the waitress directed me to sit down at a table where a young Chinese girl was seated. In America, such pairing is not practiced.

As the waitress did not speak English, the girl took on the role of translator. This is how our relationship began. I gained a beautiful city guide. First she took me to a Chinese market and persuaded me to eat a fruit called durian. It is the size of a melon, and in the middle, when cut, there are smaller fruits, which evoke some unappetizing associations with unhatched chicks. But as a real-world man who is not afraid of any exotic dishes, I ate bravely. Durian is tasty, even harsh with rum, and unlike any other fruit I know. The young Chinese woman knew how to choose something that this white man had never eaten.

She was a high school student, but she had a lot of education. She made an appointment with me to explore the city further the next afternoon. Incidentally, English is the language of instruction in Singapore, although Chinese is widely spoken.

She chose brilliantly again, because thanks to her I was able to see the Chinese district during the celebration of the Moon Festival. There were lots of stalls and lots of cakes and roasted slices of meat of different flavors. I tried a bit of everything, and then we went to the tea room. As was customary, we had to take off our shoes and sit on a mat at a low table. The Chinese have an almost religious attitude toward tea; they consider it a drink that improves digestion which must be drunk without any additives, such as sugar or lemon. The waiter brought us dry tea and boiling water in a jug and cups. He explained what brewing was and left us alone. The tea provided was strong and aromatic. We drank it for a long time, repeatedly brewing new portions, nibbling on peanuts, and chatting. We ended the evening in an open-air restaurant, where there was a barbecue and a great crowd of guests. It also had its exotic charm for me.

We met again to sail to Sandos Island, a famous entertainment destination. To be clear, my acquaintance with the young Chinese woman was purely touristic and ended with a nice "Bye bye" without even mentioning addresses. From what she said, she had a boyfriend.

On the island, which can be reached by boat in half an hour, there are various museums and a wonderful exotic zoo, and they dance to the music of the fountain. I have a video from this trip, but it is unfortunate that while I was filming sharks in the aquarium, my camera battery ran out. The shark aquarium was entered via a moving walkway through a transparent tunnel. It was an amazing experience.

Then I went to Sandos a second time, by cable car for a change, but alone. The wagons travel one hundred meters above the surface of the water, and it was in such circumstances that I met three Arab-looking men. And that was at the time of the war with Iraq. *Well*, I thought, *beautiful, I will fly like a bird in a moment, and I will end up in the sea, after my clothes and the camera show that I am an American.* They asked me where I was from, and I replied that I was a Polish American from California, not to conceal the Americanness that was dangerous at this point, but because I always answer that way.

I was flying from Singapore to Hong Kong. I ordered a 5:00 a.m. wake-up call and a taxi to the airport. I decided to try the transformer I bought in Singapore with the inscription "for dryers," to see whether it would allow the use of an American 120V hair dryer. Singapore has European voltage, 220V, and the effect was that after a few minutes, both the transformer and the hair dryer burned out. Well, I had less luggage after that.

My supplier, Fred, was waiting for me in Hong Kong. I was his guest throughout my stay. We talked about business in elegant restaurants. In Hong Kong, I found the food and service to be among the best in the world. A clean tablecloth was placed in front of each new visitor, so one didn't have to be so careful about spills. It had an atmosphere of ease and freedom. Tea was drunk before eating to improve digestion, and then waiters—two or three of them—brought platters of various dishes. There were six or seven of these dishes, and each person put as much as he wanted into small bowls. Everything was exceptionally tasty, especially meat and vegetables. Alcohol, on the other hand, was almost absent; there was only beer, and it was consumed only in the evening.

The only problem arose when the kind and hospitable Chinese wanted to teach me to eat with chopsticks, but eventually I learned the skill.

My supplier ran a typically small family business, employing almost exclusively his relatives. I noticed that the cooperation was harmonious among them, which means that in Hong Kong, families do well not only in pictures. Such honest work with the whole family in business strengthens family and financial ties; we Poles must learn this.

The city is dominated by concrete, steel, and glass. Owing to the lack of land, the streets were narrow and the houses were tall skyscrapers that soared into the sky. The roads were crowded, and the drivers showed great dexterity. I traveled around Hong Kong on the top of the tram, where I was shooting a movie with my own ongoing commentary. And all the time, I was wondering what would happen after this capitalist enclave was annexed by China. Would China begin to resemble Hong Kong or, God forbid, the other way around? Unfortunately, today everything indicates that most of the business and capital will flee abroad, likely to California. So we are in for a flood of Chinese—talented, hardworking, and enterprising people. After the Japanese influx, this may be a new, difficult competition.

I ended my stay by signing a contract for the delivery of a full container for about $20,000. Several other traders joined this shipment, with radios and watches.

The next stage of my trip was China. I immediately felt that I was in a different regime when the Chinese airline canceled my booking for no reason. Their arrogance and abrupt attitude toward the customer left me feeling as if I had been splashed with a bucket of cold water.

In order not to get into discussions with them, I bought a first-class ticket with an additional payment.

In Guangzhou, while I was exchanging money, a man approached me and offered to drive me to the hotel in a private car. I let him earn and, at the same time, learned some language about an unfamiliar city. The hotel was elegant and half the price of similar hotels in capitalist countries. In front of the entrance, there was a policeman who made sure that prostitutes did not enter. This practically meant that no single Chinese woman could be allowed in there.

After checking in, I went out to the city. I saw most of the of residents using bicycles. There were also quite a few people sleeping in the streets and begging. When I gave alms to a little girl, the whole crowd of begging children gave me away, so that I had to fight them off. Chinese people had adopted attitudes toward customers similar to those of their compatriots in Hong Kong. By that I mean they treated customers with great respect. But they probably bargained more. They could negotiate for five cents apiece for hours. It was five cents here and five cents there, and when large transactions were made, they bargained for larger sums; it was not irrational stinginess on their part. In the end, I agreed to buy a delivery of leather shoes after buying some twelve-dollar art and some Nike sportswear for ten dollars.

I stayed in Guangzhou a few days, and then I flew to Shanghai on domestic Chinese airlines. The airport in Guangzhou was so crowded that I had nowhere to put my luggage. It was quite similar in Shanghai. However, the one billion people could be felt at every step.

Shanghai is the center of business, and it shows from the moment you book your hotel at the airport. There was nothing cheaper than the $120 American five-star Holiday Inn. Whether I wanted it or not, I tried the luxury option, but the next day I changed to another hotel. The Holiday Inn was a bit off the beaten track, and I wanted to live downtown.

There was a park near the hotel; only tickets were allowed. I went for a walk there and was accosted by a group of Chinese. They asked me about various things in English because they were a group of students and they cared about the lively conversation. I had a little chat with them but immediately asked them to leave me alone. Two pretty young Chinese women did not quit and kept me company. They offered to show me around the city. Eventually, twenty-five-year-old Lili, a physics teacher by profession, became my guide. She went everywhere with me, even to my business meetings.

Later it turned out that she wanted to go to the States, but unfortunately I couldn't help this lonely girl much. Once, the American consul in Warsaw told me that we do not accept single girls to America because they break marriages. Life in China was not too sweet for Lili, because five people with her family lived in a modest, small apartment. I was in this apartment for dinner, I met Lila's brother and parents, and in return for good-bye, I threw a party in the restaurant.

I ended my travels to the Far East with a week's stay in Taiwan. There I met a very nice young man named Kuang, who showed me everything worth visiting. So I saw the so-called China Wall—that is, miniaturized China. Everything was depicted to scale: buildings, railroads, airports. I also saw a big Buddha statue on top of a mountain between the city and the coast. Nearby, there was a Buddhist chapel with a swastika on it. It was there that I found out that the Nazis had stolen this oriental symbol, which in their understanding meant rule over the world, in the Buddhist religion it symbolizes the sun.

Taiwan has more moral slack than other Asian countries, and it even trumps America. There was more porn there, more "casual" television, and topless beaches.

Taiwan's business card is the World Trade Exchange Center—a huge complex of buildings with permanent exhibitions and regularly held world exhibitions. I think that in Poland the Palace of Culture and Science in Warsaw could be used for something similar.

I moved to Poland permanently in 1992. Later, I still traveled to the States to take care of unfinished business. I hoped to register a company faster in this way, but in the meantime, a procession awaited me: a business contract, district office, regional office, and bank account. Each decision left me waiting for weeks. When I asked the clerk about something, instead of answering, he sent me to the journal set. In the United States, similar matters are dealt with almost instantly. It's good that I am a patient man and that I know Polish. Otherwise, I would have died on this obstacle course, which was created, nota bene, only for officials. They have it in their blood because they acted similarly under the Communists. That is to say not much has changed.

They made even more trouble for me at customs when the containers I had ordered arrived. They are a real clique, these customs officials, and on top of that there are no permanent regulations or fixed rates. I purchased a list of customs tariffs and tax rates and calculated how much I must pay. Meanwhile, it turned out that they had recently increased the fees for importing toys from 7 percent to 21 percent!

Not prepared for the increased sum, I had to go get the amount due from the bank. It turned out that the bank was already closed. Then there came another difficulty and another. And the customs officer did not mind, because for each day the container was kept, he was charging me 300,000 zlote!

Eventually I had to go back to the States, and my mother picked up the container. We were supposed to run the company with my mother, and it was even supposed to be her company. Even more so than I, my mother had trade in her blood. In reborn Poland, as in her young years, she ran a shop.

There were some troubles with the place, because the owner of the premises ran things in the way Poland used to be run. The clerk from the housing department determined to whom places were to be leased, and for how much. And this meant that the best places and the most favorable terms were given to relatives, buddies of the official, and those who offered bribes. The conclusion of the contract also did not guarantee one anything, because the omnipotent clerk could terminate the lease or raise the rent.

Ultimately, I bought the pavilion in the Warszawa Śródmieście railway station complex, in the very center of the city. I paid 150 million zlote, which took much convincing. The tax office valued my shop at 350 million zlote and was demanding tax on that amount. What was worse, I was the owner only of the premises, not the land, as this belonged to the railway, and I had to pay a high lease for it.

Meanwhile, the goods shipped in containers were being stored in the basement of my relatives' house. I agreed with them on the amount for the use of the premises and renovated it at my own expense. But I had barely started the business when my cousins asked for an increase from the agreed 2 million zlote to 4 million, because everything was going up in price. Shocked by such insolence, I decided to transfer all the goods to my ex-brother-in-law's place in to Prague. I announced that I was opening a store; the inauguration was solemn.

Unfortunately, everything that followed was a series of failures. And at the end of this, a real tragedy awaited.

As the saying goes, I had one foot in Poland and the other in States. Another lawsuit with my greedy, unscrupulous ex-wife kept me overseas, and in Poland, my mother took care of matters. My girlfriend sometimes teased me because I couldn't go anywhere without my mom.

In the apartment at Wileńska Street, my mother had a fax machine, so there was no problem with communication—as long as the fax machine was not tracked by municipal telecommunications and it did not demand additional fees, of course. In the USA, you do not pay extra for using a fax machine, but in Poland, as you can see, the state wants to earn on everything: customs, taxes, rents, even phone use. And as the proverb says, "The cunning lose twice." And that's right, because many people like me give up doing business in Poland, and the fig with poppy seeds will go to the cash register instead.

So the main burden of running the company was taken on by my mother. Customs duties went up, the goods came incomplete and partly stolen (and duty and tax had to be paid on the stolen goods), so I had to send my mother dollars from America. She said she was in her element, but I knew that trading on such a scale was beyond her capability. I asked my sister and friends to help me. The sister had a lot of practice in trading, had an empty store in her house, and had an adult daughter who was out of work, but she also declined, even though I was offering 25 percent of gross sales and the market value of the goods was near $100,000.

Here I wondered how the Chinese and Jews could run family businesses but we couldn't. After the bankruptcy of the store, my mother heroically decided to trade in the bazaar, without my knowledge. The idea was to recoup at least the money frozen in the commodities.

On July 18, 1994, I received tragic news in the States: my mother was dead. She had died in a fire in the apartment where we were storing the goods. I hung up the phone and felt a wave of heat pouring through me from head to toe. I was like a wounded animal that didn't know where to hide. I was crying like a baby. I felt guilty. Why did I let my mother take on this business venture in Poland? Why wasn't I with her?

Then, as I realized what the cause of my unhappiness was, my guilt grew. After all, the fire occurred from a short circuit in the wall lamp wires. I, an electrical engineer, had seen these wires with crumpled installation and—nothing. The stored goods were under the ceiling. These were flammable goods, because toys are made of plastic! My mother came back tired from work, turned on the light, and went to take a bath. Meanwhile, the room was already on fire; it was already ablaze. Mom smelled it, but it was too late. When she opened the warehouse door, smoke puffed out at her and she passed out.

I went to Poland for the funeral. I bought a granite monument, invited everyone present at the cemetery to a restaurant, and paid all the funeral costs, but it gave me no satisfaction. I took the family disputes over my mother's coffin as another nightmare.

Relatives showed me with disgusting greed what was due to them, and I agreed to accommodate them for the sake of peace. It's hard to believe that the people I had known for years behaved like hyenas, to the point where they even stole my mother's money, and mine. Immediately after the accident, they searched the apartment and found $5,000, which my mother had been keeping for a rainy day.

After these experiences, I knew that I no longer had a family in Poland. But the country still interests me vividly. I support Poles on their way to a highly developed economy, and whenever an opportunity arises, it turns on willingly.

CHAPTER 7

THE USA AND JAPAN: A COMPARISON OF THE TWO GREATEST POWERS

★ ★ ★

The United States and Japan have different cultures, different traditions, and even different understandings of basic business concepts, such as contracts, companies, and management.

American power was created by the Christian ethics of individualism. Japan's strength lies in its collaboration rooted in Confucius's teachings. It was Western specialists who laid the cornerstone for the construction of a modern, industrial Japanese economy, but its further development, almost to the point of perfection, is to the merit of the Japanese themselves. It is worth knowing that Japan practiced *Aku* from the very beginning of its endeavors into capitalism and invested more than America and Europe.

In general, in the West the term "invest" is taken to refer to the construction and modernization of factories, the financing of works related to new technologies, and the implementation of scientific achievements in the production process.

The Japanese, on the other hand, added a human worker, who is a member of the studio collective, as an investment element. In the Japanese economy, employment is practiced for life (i.e., an employee devotes his entire professional life to the same company, constantly learning and improving).

The West has a different approach there. People are interchangeable; they are hired and fired depending on production needs.

In Europe and America, the employee has a contract with the company; in Japan, the employee has attachment and a sense of belonging. Each Japanese factory is like a village housing estate where people, outside of work, lead a social life and are proud to belong.

Now I will point out a few basic differences in the functioning of the American and Japanese economies.

In the USA, trained professionals are hired to perform specific tasks, while in Japan, "the whole person" is employed, preferably fresh out of school, whom the company will train over time to perform different activities and who will probably be made into a "company man" for the rest of his life.

In America, when the management of a corporation needs investment, it sells shares. It has to show a profit to shareholders every quarter, so it focuses mainly on quarterly (i.e., short-term) profit.

Japanese management mainly thinks about long-term plans, the implementation of which is not restrained by anyone, because their investments come from long-term loans from a bank.

American management feels most responsible to shareholders, and Japanese management to employees. You can make money either way, but the planning is different.

American trade unions have a federal structure, so when a conflict with an employer occurs in New York, for example, strikes break out simultaneously in Boston, Chicago, and other cities where the union has influence. By contrast, Japanese trade unions are closely tied to one company and defend only the interests of their employees.

In Japan, as in America, business breeds conflict, but these conflicts rarely see an epilogue in court. America, the country of millions of lawyers, is drowning in a flood of lawsuits, and the Japanese, among whom there are no more than thirty thousand lawyers, somehow manage to get along.

The Japanese government is limited to the role of a consultant and does not interfere with the economy to the same extent as the American administration.

The American director wants to rule and lead the people; the Japanese director thinks primarily about building a collective, and he encourages his people to make decisions that he later approves or rejects for amendment.

The American worker waits to be told what to do; the Japanese worker, who has been given a share of the leadership, happily enriches the collective with his own initiative. The latter difference results not only from national assessments but also to a large extent from the fact that education in Japan (both general and vocational) is at a higher level than education in the USA.

America relies on outstanding individuals; Japan relies on harmoniously educated masses. It is interesting that in recent decades, Japan has avoided the main ills that plague America regarding economic development: stagnation, unemployment, income stratification, and the atomization of society. America, instead of looking to the future, looks toward the receding fruitful past and cannot shake off such thinking.

A problem for politicians in the United States is election and re-election, hence their philosophy of giving people more and more without requiring anything in return, even simple responsibility for the economy and the country. At the same time as the

US government was squandering money on idle programs, the Japanese government was generating new industrial development and modernizing existing industry, making bold plans to win markets. This momentum and optimism fuel the Japanese economy to this day.

In Japan, every company and every industrial plant is like a political unit. As an association of people, it cares about the expansion of the market, prestige in the eyes of society and abroad, and good interpersonal relations within the company. The mentality and style of action of the Japanese manager are characterized by three elements: (1) focusing on people as an important resource, (2) awareness that the company is an environment, and (3) focus on constant growth.

This focus on people determines the overall relationship between management and staff, starting with employment policy. When I took my first steps in America as an immigrant, I was often puzzled by the question of the meaning of the experience requirement forever quoted in job advertisements. For me it was an example of an absurd, vicious circle—after all, the experience could only be gained by working in a given profession, and because no businesses would accept employees without experience, then something seemed wrong. People like me—immigrants, or people fresh out of school—went through a vicious cycle because of this.

In Japan, we would not have to do this, because there freshmen are most desired by companies. If they want to make him a company man for life, then, of course, they prefer a young person, a kind of tabula rasa, to an older one who is perhaps burdened with bad habits, which unfortunately often boils down to the so-called work experience.

A newly hired Japanese has a long career ahead of him, with numerous promotions conditioned by seniority. This perspective makes him resistant to any temptation to change jobs.

Of course, lifelong employment is often excessive employment, for which employers pay extra. But the government does not have to pay unemployment benefits for this. When an employee is involved, Japanese management looks not only at his education but also at his character. This is followed by intensive professional and moral training (i.e., learning conscientiousness, compliance, and friendly cooperation). For three to six months, the new employee is closely monitored to make sure that he or she is working professionally and ethically—especially ethically!

This preference is quite understandable here. In an individualistic America, one can tolerate a bastard if he is a good specialist. In a collectivized Japanese system, the black sheep must be eliminated for the sake of the common good.

As I have already mentioned, employment in Japan is usually lifelong. If necessary, the employee is reclassified to a different position, and even having reached retirement age, he often maintains contact with the company by performing various commissioned work for it. HR offices have enormous power; they decide about employee transfers within the organization, and they award promotions based on age, achievements, seniority, and family status.

There is no such thing as a contract, as contracts are understood by American reasoning, in Japan. Everything is based on mutual commitment and loyalty. It is a pity that these words in America mean so little today that the management of the companies, not feeling the slightest loyalty to the staff in difficult times, increase their salaries when wages are falling.

It is unthinkable in Japan. When wages in the company go down, the first people to take pay cuts are the management.

In America, management doesn't care about seniority, and it's just as easy to lay off beginners as it is those who have worked in the company for twenty years. In Japan, there can be no question about this, as it removes the stress for employees related to the fear of dismissal and at the same time, contrary to the popular argument of supporters of unemployment, does not demoralize them. Even at the very peak of his career, say after thirty years of work, someone who knows he will definitely be fired does his job with the same diligence as young person during the trial period.

In both American and Japanese companies, boxes are installed in which employees can put cards with their suggestions written on them. But in the USA, 14 percent of employees use this form of comanagement, and in Japan the figure is 54 percent. Moreover, Japanese management takes these suggestions into account to a much greater extent.

The awareness that the company is in a local environment is very strong in Japan. A housing estate is a company, and all social events take place around it. The environment, understood in this way, is not only the focus of all social activities (until retirement, because after retirement, the care of the former employee is taken over by the government) but also a place for the formation of initiatives and even economic decisions. In the Japanese economy, as in the Japanese army, the decisions go from the ground up. And at the top is responsibility. Through numerous meetings and discussions, a new production plan is drawn up. Everyone contributes ideas and comments, and only the final document is submitted to the director's desk for approval.

Japanese corporate presidents are educated at the country's best universities. As a rule, they have many years of work in corporations behind them and are a long way up the career ladder. They have great authority; for example, getting into the president's office is almost like getting an audience with a monarch. And yet the greats of the Japanese economy charge an average annual salary of $400,000, which is four times less than their American counterparts. The Japanese president of a corporation does not live an exclusive life, he lives in a house not much better than those of his employees, and when difficult times come, he is the first to reduce his salary.

The Japanese president of a corporation is closely tied to one industry and one company, while American businessmen shuffle, as the economic situation changes, from electronics to banking, from banking to kerosene, and so forth. Thus they neglects long-term planning.

It seems that the Japanese orientation toward people and the environment gives better results than the American perception of only the market and its indicators in the economy, which is supposedly supported by science.

Growth orientation of management is significantly different from US profit-seeking. In the USA, they say, "Profit is the name of the game" (i.e., profit is the main motive of business operations).

Meanwhile, the Japanese do not consider profit an end in itself. For them, the development of the production environment is important. If you produce good things, new things, this will create demand, and the profit will come by itself.

A Pole who reminisces about central planning with disgust will be surprised to learn that five-year plans are fashionable in Japan. There is a general belief that companies can join together and undertake a joint development plan. This has nothing to do, I reassure the Polish reader, with planning a la Hilary Minc. Japan's years-long rule by the Liberal Democratic Party has nothing to do with the Communists; the nation is very deserving of its development.

The Japanese economic miracle of the post-war forties was largely planned. It was created, and generated by people and institutions acting collectively and harmoniously. History has taught them that fragmentation and dissolution, where everyone pulls his own way, leads to nothing.

A strong work ethic is deeply rooted in Japanese tradition. It is the capitalist ethos today that is largely based on Confucianism (a Chinese belief system imported to Japan in the fourth century), which teaches brotherhood, respect for elders, ancestors, the law, and fair conduct. For the followers of Confucius, honest interpersonal intercourse is more important than a mystical deity.

Of course, in Japan, there are also other religions, such as Buddhism and, in the minority, Christianity. Generally, however, the Japanese do not have their own deity, but they adhere very strictly to the ethical standards, the basis of which they inherited from religion.

Buddhism is a religion without a god to believe in. This religion, founded in India in the fifth century before the birth of Christ, had the task of making a person spiritually free and connecting him spiritually to the heavens. Achieving the climax in this religion—that is, the release of the body from pain, the separation of the mind from the body—is achieved through correct life, meditation, and, in extreme cases, ascetic methods, such as fasting for several days, pouring cold water on oneself, or whipping. This was mainly done by Buddhist monks who lived in humiliation while begging.

From ordinary mortals and the followers of Buddhism, only positive character was expected. This meant avoiding aggressive behavior and measures that stimulated or darkened the mind, observing holy days and festivals, and fulfilling obligations for society as a good student, parent, employee, neighbor, and friend (i.e., living an honest life).

Japanese Buddhism underwent many transformations and merged with the national Japanese religion of Shinto, and the two religions coexisted in Japan. Buddhism was the religion of the Japanese aristocracy. A branch of Buddhism called Zen was designed for developmental and physical discipline and became the religion of the samurai, who played a huge role in the nation for six hundred years. As Buddhism became the religion of the masses, corruption and abuse of power became widespread, and ancient teachings were pushed aside.

When Christian missionaries came to Japan in the sixteenth

century, the Japanese listened willingly, but as a result of the political and financial machinations of Portuguese priests, Catholic teachers had to leave Japan.

In the nineteenth century, during the renewal, Buddhism was recognized as a religion of violence by local authorities and Emperor Meiji, and it was forbidden to practice it. It was then that the native Shinto religion was elevated to the national religion. Strong influences of Buddhism remain, and the pursuit of self-enlightenment, attainable by fully recognizing the essence of life and reality, has become the basis of thinking. The goal of Buddhism is to eliminate feelings of jealousy and hatred through boundless love. This religion says that nothing is eternal. The core of faith is tolerance and equality. Buddhism contains elements of life derived from nature, harmonious coexistence that keeps society from falling apart, and elements of democracy that give it strength. The Japanese accepted everything that made sense, which could be logically and reasonably explained. The whole concept of Japanese capitalism was based on this.

The Shinto religion brought humans very close to nature, which is considered a kind of mother of all people. This faith is based on a strong love and attachment to nature, without which humans cannot live. Maybe it was the Shinto belief system that allowed the Japanese to adapt to the industrial and technical world, which they mastered to perfection in a very short time. This religion recognizes only what is pure; it does not recognize the devil, and it considers death and decaying bodies to be the dirtiest things.

The Japanese believe in reincarnation (i.e., rebirth after death). One becomes cleansed by washing in the sea, in a river, or under a waterfall, of by washing one's hands and mouth in a religious fountain. A paper tape or a rope is hung over the cleaned person or thing. These rites have made the Japanese the cleanest nation in the world. We can observe this on a daily basis, in the form of clean sushi bars and in the Japanese love of taking hot baths every day. The Shinto religion dates back to the time when epidemics decimated the Japanese people.

In the middle of the nineteenth century, there was no industry in Japan yet, while France, Germany, and England did have industry. A close relationship between the government and business began to emerge. There was no capital for investment, and the government established a tax system and created the National Bank of Japan. In this way, the inflowing money was controlled, and a strong dependence of business on bank financing was born, which still exists today.

Modern, industrialized Japan began in the nineteenth century. It can be said that the restoration carried out during the reign of Emperor Meiji (1852–1912) marked a new era for Japan. From a feudal samurai state divided and cut off from the world, the Land of the Rising Sun began to turn into an economic and local power.

The main motive that led the leaders of the time to break the three-hundred-year isolation of Japan and carry out Western-style industrialization was the fear of Western and Russian imperialism. A significant document of this period is the emperor's five-point manifesto (issued on behalf of the emperor) stating that

- decisions on important issues must be made after deep social discussions with the participation and support of society as a whole,
- all strata of society—high and low—must unite to jointly support the country's administrative affairs,
- ordinary people have the same rights as officials and officers,
- the devilish laws of the past were giving way to the just laws of nature, and
- knowledge is to be searched out all over the world to strengthen the empire.

In 1871, a delegation of Japanese high officials traveled west to find out about the progress of the Industrial Revolution. They realized that they were fifty years behind, as they had no railroads, no telegraphs, and no steamboats. They realized that only through study and work could they catch up with the rest of the world.

Fukuzawa was a famous teacher during the period of renewal. He was the son of a poor samurai, was fluent in English, and was fascinated by Western civilization. For many years he did not leave his home before dark, fearing an attack by opponents of Europeanization. In 1860, he was sent to America and Europe. Upon his return, he wrote a three-volume book, *Conditions in the West*, which made him famous.

He was a supporter of parliamentarism, universal education, language reform, and the improvement of the status of Japanese women. He founded an institute that educated a whole generation of future leaders of the Japanese economy. As a teacher, he wrote that thanks to nature, all people are equal at birth, but the difference between wisdom and stupidity lies in education.

Another one who contributed greatly to the Japanese renewal was Shibusawa, the farmer's son, who was the minister of finance in the Emperor Meiji government. He was known for his honesty and intransigent hostility regarding corruption and ignorance. From the newly enriching businessmen he was required to care for the general interest of the state and proclaimed that profit was not the main motive in the economy, but the good of the company, people, and country. Shibusawa dedicates these words to young Polish capitalism!

During the renewal period, two slogans dominated in Japan: "Enrich the country!" and "Strengthen the army!" The main goal was industrialization. The Meiji government built factories and sold them into private hands, mostly into the hands of Samurai who were willing to take the risk. The first significant investment was the launch of a silk factory with the help of the French.

The government attached so much importance to this undertaking that it allowed only women from samurai families to be employed in the production. In a short time, the export of silk allowed for the further—as we would say today—purchase of Western technology. As I mentioned, the government sold factories into private hands, but as long as they remained state-owned, they were not profit-oriented but served training purposes. In general, Japanese heavy industry was created thanks to state money.

The Japanese countryside paid for the development of the industry. The government of that time was a categorical opponent of lending money abroad. Industry taxation was very low, to encourage initiative and experimentation.

The rise in taxes even sparked a rebellion among the peasants. However, the resistance was broken, and as compensation farmers received government aid and a reward system for the modernization of farms and the implementation of modern methods of poultry farming.

The next leap in the Japanese economy of this magnitude, comparable to the Meiji revival, took place after World War II and is often referred to as the "Japanese economic miracle." It must be made clear that this miracle, apart from the talent and diligence of the Japanese, was greatly contributed to by the American occupation. Without the draconian rationing of the Dodge Plan in 1949, and without the supplies to the US military in Korea, which gave Japan $3 billion, it would probably have been difficult to start the postwar economy of the Land of Cherry Blossoms.

In addition, the Japanese owe the Americans for their democratization, which came about as a result of the force imposed by the troops of McArthur.

Huge corporations formed, as did the so-called zaibatsu, and land reform was carried out, and all citizens were legally guaranteed an equal start. And since the Japanese were willing to learn and work hard, they started hard!

Under Emperor Meiji, Japan's consultants were specialists from Europe, and after World War II, the consultants were the Americans.

The Japanese tax system—which incidentally, being too modern, was not adopted in the States—was created by a professor from Columbia University.

The Japanese were taught statistical quality control by Edward Deming, and this is interesting: in Japan, Deming's teachings have been used for a long time. There is even a prestigious award named after him for product quality. Yet in America we are only taking the first steps in implementing statistical quality control!

Between 1955 and 1970, the Japanese bought American licenses for $2.7 billion. If instead of selling technology we had entered Japan with our own product, establishing branches or limited liability companies, the market of this country would not be hermetically closed to us today, and we would not have such a powerful competitor in the Japanese.

As an example, the transistor, invented in American military laboratories, was sold in 1954 to Sony. Sony developed low-cost production methods to satisfy civilian needs and flooded global markets with commercial electronics.

In 1950, the Ministry of International Trade and Industry was established in Tokyo. It was a strange institution in that it operated in the capitalist system and aimed at its development, while at the same time it was an institution of the martial law government.

Young bureaucrats and businessmen worked together to develop a strategic five-year plan to rebuild the industry. Then the focus was on individual branches. This is how the project of cooperation between government and business was created, which is in force in Japan to this day.

Generally, the Japanese adopt a strategy of focusing on one branch of industry, improving the product as much as possible, and winning the market for it. They don't always succeed on the first try. The first Toyota brought to America turned out to be a failure; it had difficulty going uphill on the California slopes. But the Japanese did not give up, analyzed the mistakes, and finally won our car market.

They were good students. Managers taught their subordinates—a method neglected in America. Japanese cars (which were then better than American ones) were priced lower than American cars. Customers started buying them and got used to Japanese cars. Today they cannot really get used to it, even though the quality of Japanese and American machines is now comparable and the prices of Japanese cars are higher.

The scourge of the eighties in America was the so-called unfriendly purchase of shares (i.e., the buying out of one company by another). Later, management was taken over, and of course, entire departments were closed, and hence employees were dismissed. Company X, instead of expanding the market, establishing branches, and generally developing, achieved its goals by buying and destroying the weaker Company Y and Company Z. In that way, competition was eliminated, but these and similar practices were obviously not healthy for the country's economy. Only the lawyers servicing the legal side of such transactions benefited from this.

In Japan, the unfriendly purchase of a small company by a large one is not accepted. The government opposes such transactions. Japanese law allows for any form of merger only after two-thirds of the owners of the shares of both companies have agreed. This philosophy comes from the fact that for the Japanese government, the Japanese company consists of people to be reckoned with. In the USA, however, companies are viewed only as real estate being sold.

In the past, in America, only hired directors sat on the boards of corporations (in Japan this is the case today). Now outsiders have also been included, most often deserving and enjoying public trust but not having the slightest idea what is going on in the corporations.

"Why do you hire such people?" A Japanese businessman might ask an American businessman. The answer is that he does so because it increases the trust of shareholders.

If the shareholders do not trust the directors, then maybe, instead of employing some people from the outside, they will feel that the managerial board should be replaced. When a Japanese businessman learns that the boards of corporations are controlled by a government agency called the Securities and Exchange Commission, he expresses his amazement that the American government has nothing better to do.

In Japan, it is simply assumed that corporate directors have the interests of their shareholders in mind and that Japanese trust seems to work better than US control. As I said, there are, of course, conflicts in Japan ("Without conflicts, there is no progress," said the president of a large Japanese corporation), but the Japanese have a much higher degree of compromise. And in Japan, both A and B are included, and thus there are no winners or losers and all winners.

In the 1980s, a Japanese worker worked an average of 43.5 hours a week, while an American worker worked 37.3 hours and a German worker 37.2 hours. Wages rose faster in Japan. Between 1972 and 1980, the hourly wage of a Japanese worker increased from 422 yen to 1,090 yen (about 100 yen = 1 US dollar), or from $4.13 to $7.96.

In the 1980s, 31 percent of Japanese-employed persons belonged to trade unions (in the USA this figure was 23 percent; in Great Britain, 57.4 percent; and in Germany and Czechoslovakia, 41.9 percent), but nevertheless, the loss of time caused by strikes was incomparably lower there than in other industrialized countries. For example, in 1977, the US industry lost 33 million robot-day trips to strikes, and Japanese less than a million. A similar proportion was maintained in the following years.

The American worker says he goes to work, and the Japanese worker says he goes to the company. This small linguistic nuance has enormous consequences: the Japanese feel that they are part of their enterprise, which is their environment. This pertains not only to professional endeavors but also to life. Of course, the workers' union operates in this environment, but its purpose is to protect only its own. And it is such protection that will not affect the environment itself (i.e., the company).

There is a simple calculation: if the firm does not make money, neither do the workers. Japanese executives and workers know that the success of all is built upon the company's success, and the never allow it to destroy the company, as is often the case in the West.

American unions control entire industries from the Atlantic to the Pacific and from Mexico to Canada. Their leaders, from their heights, are not able to see any single company. If they order a strike, it is nationwide. Thus, a conflict, which in Japan would end in a reasonable compromise at the enterprise level, engulfs the entire economy in our country, paralyzing it for many days and weeks and causing unimaginable losses.

In Japan, disputes (within the company under the heading) between the union and the employer seem to be family-type disputes. There is goodwill on both sides to reach a compromise and, above all, not to endanger the company. The parties sit down opposite each other (the union side with red bands on their foreheads) and, with pencils in hand, determine how feasible it is to raise wages, housing benefits, educational benefits, and the like.

The management of the corporation, however, does not call the police even then. As a rule, it is forewarned internally by the company's intelligence about the mood of the crew, and before any excesses occur, the management discreetly leaves the skyscraper. In Japan, strikes are legally prohibited by the state administration, because it has a fixed budget that no one and nothing can change.

After the war, the US occupation authorities introduced a Western-style educational system in Japan. Schools were taken over by local authorities, and the role of the Ministry of Education was reduced to advisory services. Ethics was removed from the primary school curriculum, replaced by a number of characteristics of American so-called liberal teaching. So the students chose classes and subjects that interested them, just as in the USA. These novelties were massively criticized. It was believed that the new system undermined discipline, parental authority, and even national and moral values. Finally, strict conservatism rejected the change, and today in Japan the ministry directs education, and ethics is back on the agenda.

The undisputed superiority of Japanese education indicates that this was the right step.

I consider it a great achievement for the Japanese that they found a way to obey the law without lawyers. A Japanese proverb says. "In quarrels, no two parties are to blame." Another says, "Rule the people by law and land them sharply for their offenses, they will lose respect for each other and run away from you, and rule them with moral powers and strengthen them in them these forces will regain self-respect and will cling to you of their own free will."

There are thirty thousand lawyers in Japan and seven hundred thousand in America. In America, every fourth citizen complains or is accused himself. In Japan, most people live their whole lives without ever seeing a court or a lawyer. The same applies to criminal law. Data for 1973 say that in Tokyo there were 186 murders and 1,680 rapes; in New York, there were 426 and 3,735, respectively. There were 3,555 car thefts in Tokyo and 82,731 in New York. Japanese criminal statistics are also favorable as compared to those of Europe.

Yet Japanese criminal law is less restrictive than American law; in the Japanese tradition, order is maintained more through

the development of morality than through regulations and re-
pression. In minor matters, it is obligatory to seek consensus and
redress, and the only ones considered villains are those who refuse
to compensate for damage caused. Of course, in serious cases,
there are severe penalties.

Japanese contracts include a clause that in the event of dis-
agreement the parties should discuss matters with each other in
good faith. Unlike Japanese contracts, our contracts are stiff.

Business negotiations in America always take place in the
presence of the parties' attorneys, which above all is intended to
give them the necessary prestige; the party who comes to negotiate
without a lawyer shows no serious attitude toward the case.

In Japan, on the contrary, if someone comes with an attorney,
he immediately exposes himself to the suspicion that his intentions are not pure—that, to put it bluntly, he is going to use legal
tricks to screw the contractor. In America, every corporation has
its own legal department; in Japan, this is rare. Of course, in negotiating with the Americans—"Entering among the crows ..."—
the Japanese hire lawyers, but only foreign ones. Talking to an
American corporation without a lawyer is like walking in Central
Park at midnight. You run the risk of getting hit in the head and
losing your money!

Being surrounded by attorneys in America is not just friv-
olousness, but a necessity. Our business, and indeed our lives,
have become so engrossed in a web of rules and regulations that
ordinary mortals feel stupid and helpless. And lawyers rub their
hands as they earn $150 to $250 an hour!

The occupying American authorities tried to introduce a number of our legal regulations in Japan after the war, but the Japanese
dealt with that similarly to the imposed educational reform (i.e.,
they rejected it). Today, cooperation between the Japanese government and Japanese business is harmonious, and lawyers are
not needed. Lawyers are also not needed in Japanese tax matters,

which, as you know, is the basis of some lawyers' incomes in the United States. It looks as if our tax law was written by lawyers using their esoteric language so that no one could understand it on their own and would have to refer all the time—for a fee—to their enlightened advice. In Japan, tax matters are dealt with between the company's accounts and the local tax office based on simple, generally understandable rules and without intermediaries.

In Japan, when one party wants to renegotiate a contract, it will first end deals with the other party; in America, this process starts with consultation with an attorney (or, in the case of large companies, with a legal department), whether or not changes to one's advantage can be obtained with legal trickery. We have made the law a deity in Europe and America. It regulates the overall relationship between government and society, as well as between citizens. A Japanese writer even noted that Western culture had downright "harnessed" God to legal acts by introducing the obligation to swear in his name, introducing him as if he is an indisputable third party. The Japanese believe that a contract is a "good faith contract" between imperfect beings, such as humans, to be discussed at any time.

Unlike us, the Japanese seem to treat the law as a necessary evil. They would probably most willingly go back to the good old way of getting things done on a promise and a handshake.

Paradoxically, a Japanese, in his approach to law adheres to the teachings of Christ to a greater extent than a Christian. Let us recall: "Let your speech be: yes and no; everything that is too much comes from evil."

In Japan, the state bureaucracy has traditionally played a large and positive role. To become a high official, you need a thorough education and must also pass a difficult competitive exam.

For example, in 1980, only thirteen hundred were accepted for from among fifty thousand graduates who applied for government jobs. The most prestigious work is at the Ministry of Finance, followed closely by the Ministry of Foreign Affairs, the Ministry of Industry and Foreign Trade. And what's interesting—it's all about prestige, because they are at the top of the social ladder. After all, the salaries in administration are not stunning, or at least are much lower than in normal business. And yet a state official stays in the position and goes to the private sector only after retirement. In Japan, the middle official has more responsibility and power than in the United States. He is a direct link between the government and business, influences the policy of the ministry, and often creates plans himself and leads to their approval by the sovereignty.

When, after years of work, such an official is promoted to the position of deputy minister, all his classmates must resign. The point is that the service pragmatics should not be disturbed by various awkward situations.

Contrary to the American one, the Japanese ministry does not interfere in the economy and does not influence the legislature to issue new, often burdensome regulations. His job is to set a strategic goal, control inflation, support the development of profitable divisions, and switch to a different type of nonprofit division production.

In the 1950s, the Ministry of Industry and Foreign Trade influenced the computer industry to conduct research together with government laboratories. As a result, Japanese computer companies are competing with American ones today! In the 1950s and 1960s, when the Japanese industry was still developing, MITI protected the domestic market much more than it does today. Currently, it has a significant impact on the actions of the auto industry; it recommends Japanese automotive companies to reduce exports and encourages the construction of factories in the USA.

Private industry is not always willing to follow the ministry's recommendations, and officials then have to resort to indirect pressure. For example, in a recession, it can set up cartels, or clusters of companies, to regulate output and prices, forcing small businesses to come together and making the market looser. In America, such action would be illegal.

In the USA, close cooperation between industry and government exists only in the area of armaments. In Japan, such cooperation also exists in the economy that usually pursues commercial, civilian goals. And so the Japanese government switched the limping textile industry to another, more modern and more profitable, mode of production. The chemical industry was also strengthened thanks to state subsidies.

The economically advantageous merger of car companies was also initiated by a government initiative. (Not all car companies agreed to this merger, but this is a separate matter.) The state also provides scientific aid; it is in government laboratories that Japanese computers and semiconductors have been improved, as well as jet engines and airplanes, which were another government priority. The government helps the industry by guaranteeing loans and cutting taxes, which is especially the case when it comes to investment and exports.

The showcase of the Japanese economy is, among other areas, steel production.

The production logic is not native to the Japanese, yet Japan is one of the world's largest producers. The steel plant in Ichishima, built for $4 billion, is the most modern in the world. Everything has been automated in it; its lifts, furnaces, and transport vehicles work without the slightest human intervention. There are no grimy steelworkers, just a few engineers in the control tower.

Forty years ago, Japan bought steel equipment from the United States; today they can be a teacher to the steelmakers of Pittsburgh, Gary, and Bethlehem. Investing in modernity pays off, as you can see. The fact is that the plant in Ichishima was twice as expensive as a traditional steel plant, but the operating cost is cheaper—three times so! Japan, which did not even have its own ore in the 1960s, was producing half the quantity of steel as the United States; in 1980 it was already producing 25 percent more steel than the United States.

Meanwhile, our trade unions can protest against the automation of production! It is obviously not the case that we in America are unfamiliar with modern metallurgical technologies; we simply lack the funds to implement them. And no wonder, since the annual economic growth in Japan is 6 percent and in the USA only 2 percent. America seems to live off its formerly accumulated wealth, slowly consuming it.

All industrialized countries face the problem of poisoning the natural environment, and such giants as the USA and Japan, of course, are facing the issue in a special way. There is a government agency in the USA that sues those guilty of poisoning the environment. However, this method is both costly and ineffective. Obviously, lawyers earn money, and court judgments ordering, for example, the transfer of funds from investments to environmental protection do not always seem reasonable.

Japan adopted a different strategy. The government took matters into its own hands. They began to discipline the polluters effectively. Court cases were rare; usually being pilloried by public opinion was enough. The government gave companies professional advice and tax breaks for the purchase and installation of antipollution devices. The Japanese administration had a huge arsenal of measures against the polluters and used them until a positive result was achieved.

Apart from cleanliness, the Japanese are also characterized by their economy. In this respect, they beat us and Europe over the head. In fact, saving is strongly inscribed in the Japanese national tradition, and today it is bringing about excellent economic results.

Japanese corporations, in terms of annual gross capital, save up to 40 percent, which is twice as much as Americans and

Europeans. There are also strong incentives to save. For example, prospering companies can pay their employees bonuses of three to eight salaries twice a year.

Moreover, the accumulation of savings is encouraged by the tax system, which exempts income from interest on sums deposited in banks up to the amount of 3 million yen. If someone has accumulated more, and therefore their interest rate exceeds this limit, maybe legally, and this is not a "combination," they may spread the savings over several accounts, because their interest will then not be added up. Needless to say, that much money being placed in banks is a possibility.

There are no funds for investments in the US because Americans are not saving.

Another positive feature of the Japanese is perfection. Perhaps that is why they have embraced Dr. Deming's statistical quality control system so well.

Americans admit the failure of their production on the level of 1 to 5 percent, believing that screwing a lower level does not make economic sense; the Japanese assume that it is better to produce better quality than worse, and they can set the level of control and faults even to 0.1 percent! This is possible thanks to the so-called quality control groups. These are teams of five to ten people operating at all levels of production, but above all, the lowest. It can be said that the Japanese worker—that is, the one who stands closest to the direct production process and has the best insight into it—is like a policeman-inspector, not letting his factory produce junk.

Let me not hear nonsense like this system being impossible to introduce in Poland! It can be introduced, and it would be worth it! In the United States, this system, although with a delay, is already there.

For example, it was none other than a group of thirty-five Nissan employees that automated the production of the Datsun

350 body. Now that production is six times faster than in the corresponding American factories. And Honda crashes one hundred cars an hour, a quarter more than American auto companies. This is the result of the combined effort of all staff, from the director, through the manager and master, to the worker, because when it comes to quality control, everyone is equal. This is what the Japanese can do!

In view of the popularity of many American products on the Japanese market, the permanent surplus of Japan in trade with us seems not to be very understandable. In 1981 it amounted to $18 billion, and in 1994, $60 billion.

In the 1960s, we could export factories to Japan relatively cheaply, but now it is a very expensive undertaking. This state of affairs was due to several reasons: the historic security of the Japanese market against imports and the difference in the approach to the economy of the governments of both countries.

In order for an American product to reach the Japanese market, it must undergo a long, complicated procedure of various approvals. The Japanese Tokyo Bank was able to buy California First Bank, and it has already become the owner of one hundred branches with the same rights as any American bank.

No American company could do the same in Japan. Perhaps that is due to the factor of American guilt regarding the atomic bomb. Also, as a result of US monetary policy in the 1980s, high interest rates kept the dollar high against the yen, but this state of affairs of course provided the impetus for the Japanese to locate industry in the United States. In this way, they finally conquered our market—but not without the attitude of the American customer, who, when buying, sees that the goods are good and cheap and is not interested in the producer.

Unlike us, the Japanese, as citizens, defend their nest and are not indifferent to whether they buy their own traditions or foreign ones. Ultimately, we have a situation where Japan is flooding the American market with finished products, mainly cars and electronics, which we repay by exporting food and raw materials to Japan. Unfortunately, this is a relationship between countries with different degrees of industrialization. This is how you avenge recklessness and focus on short-term profit, selling technology instead of investing in Japan—and, of course, failing to properly protect one's own market!

There is an opinion that there is an economic war between the United States and Japan, and now China. In military terms, we are opposed by an army of well-educated Japanese and Chinese (who are in first place in the world in terms of the number of educated people), strong, tight-knit, ready, and solidary. Although the Japanese compete fiercely with each other, when confronted with foreign businesses, especially American ones, they immediately unite into one camp.

The largest Japanese investment in America is the Honda motorcycle facility built in the 1980s in Columbus, Ohio, which today produces about one hundred thousand motorcycles. In 1982, Honda also began producing cars in Detroit.

There was also the purchase by Matsushita of the American company Motorola, which produces color TV sets near Chicago. In both cases, Japanese management employs Americans, but the style, methods, and philosophy of work are Japanese. Working in Japanese fashion, our compatriots are more productive and earn more. For example, the number of defects in Motorola's production under Japanese management has decreased more than twentyfold! Apparently, their philosophy of building a human team works better than ours, as expressed in the famous American saying that if you have a problem with an employee, you should fire them, and if the problem is with an employer, you should go to the competition.

I have written a lot about Japan's strengths, so I need to balance it by mentioning their main weakness. Namely, Japan has practically no army. Lying close to not very benevolent powers, such as Russia and China, it is defenseless.

But they can spend only 1 percent of the budget on armaments, while we spend as much as 8 percent—paradoxically, partially in order to defend Japan if necessary!

In order to understand Japanese society, one must realize that it is traditionally hierarchical and clan-like. Everyone has a place on the social ladder, as dictated by age, education, employment, length of service, and so forth, and almost everyone belongs to some group to which they must submit. Group interest has always stood above the individual in Japan!

Nowadays, the role of a group or a clan is taken over by the company. In 1980, as many as 73 percent of Japanese respondents replied that the company they worked for was part of their life, and they put the companies' interests on an equal footing with personal interests. Only 21 percent of the American population answered positively to the same question.

For America, China, Japan, Taiwan, South Korea, and Singapore are economic threats. Moreover, the capitalism of these countries has a similar Confucian tradition. The younger generations of these countries have already lost some of their Confucian ethics.

The Japanese have a pro-productive structure of education. Out of ten thousand Japanese, there are four hundred engineers and scientists, one lawyer, and three accountants; out of ten thousand Americans, there are seventy engineers and scientists, twenty lawyers, and forty accountants. The pattern of the "business hero" is also different in both countries.

On the other hand, they have an unfavorable demographic situation, just like us. In 1982, 11 percent of Americans and 10 percent of Japanese were over sixty-five years of age, and in both countries, the aging of the population is unfortunately increasing. As you can see, Japan also has problems and threats for the future, but there is nothing to console yourself with, because for the time being they, not us, are the world's largest exporter, and they have recently proposed providing economic aid to us (not the other way around, as has usually been the case), if you believe the *Washington Post*.

For many decades, Japan was ruled by the Liberal Democratic Party until it lost its advantage in 1993. The party supported business, which had positive consequences for Japan and its people. Nobody knew what was behind the success of this party.

It was not until 1994 that it became known that for all those years, the Liberal Democratic Party in Japan had been financially supported by the American Central Intelligence Agency. This was because America wanted a strong anti-communist Japan as a counterbalance to the spread of the socialist ideals of the Soviet Union. By the end of 1989, the threat of Communism had ceased to exist, and the CIA changed its policy toward the already strong Japan. The next candidate for American aid may be Poland, which I will describe in a later chapter.

CHAPTER 8

CONTEMPORARY POLAND

★ ★ ★

I believe that just like Japan, which in ten years rose from the ruins of the war and began rebuilding the economy to pre-1940 levels, Poland, destroyed by Communism, may become a European trade and industrial center within a decade.

The road to this destination, however, is not as simple as many may believe. A massive influx of foreign investment was expected, and here disappointment ensued. Although Poland has a relatively cheap and well-qualified workforce, which may encourage investors, the purchasing power on the market is weak because Poles earn little and therefore buy little. The land is relatively inexpensive, but there is no infrastructure in the form of efficient telecommunications, motorway networks, and so on. And above all, there are no good and stable legal regulations regarding business.

Another weakness is the fact that in Communist times, the most gifted Poles went abroad. It is a pity that nowadays little is being done to encourage them to return, and yet there are many patriots among emigrants who, after the change of the political system, willingly joined the building of the Republic of Poland.

Meanwhile, the legislation is moving in the opposite direction. Right after the first presidential election, the Sejm issued an act stating that a candidate for an important position must live in the country for five years.

The stable international and regional situation is an advantage, although of course there is no shortage of prospective threats. Russia's opposition is blocking our accession to NATO because America does not want to annoy Yeltsin and accepts his veto. However, it will not take long before Poland will join NATO. It is terrifying to think what will happen if Zhirinovsky or the like wins the elections in Russia!

America will not quickly change its course toward Russia, because the perception in America is that this is an excessive price to pay for world peace and stability. Russia, on the other hand, can change its course. I watched an interview with Zhirinovski in which he claimed that when the US bombs Sarajevo, Russia will bomb New York in retaliation. Another time he said it was time for Alaska, Finland, and Poland to return to Russia. This is probably just a psychological trick of the Russians. I had the impression that Zhirinovsky was an insane man! They probably have more talented people there!

Poland should try hard to join NATO. The events of 1939 cannot be repeated, when it was attacked almost simultaneously from the west and the east, unable to count on help from other countries. Poland must become economically stronger and live in harmony with the West and all its neighbors.

However, we have no influence on it, so let us just, as Młynarski sang, do our job. And the first step to economic success is, as the example of Japan shows, good education.

In my opinion, education in Poland should be state-run, with the simultaneous existence of private schools, which will ensure healthy competition. The same general curriculum should apply to all types of schools programs.

The Ministry of Education, which is the author of the program, must ensure that learning is "for real" (i.e., that students spend two to three hours a day doing homework, and that the promotion from class to class is determined by annual final exams). With a high level of education, the weaker students will be able to join the better ones.

Primary school education should start at six years old, while younger children, aged three and over, should be sent to kindergarten to learn the basics of reading, writing, and arithmetic. If they do not go to kindergarten, initial education should be taken care of by parents.

An important element of education is a cooperation between school and home. Parents and teachers should introduce children to honest and systematic work (both individually and collectively), because the habits developed will remain for life. Conversely, if the primary school period is neglected from the educational point of view, it is very difficult to make up for it later.

Parents need to understand (and many already do) how useful it is for a child to understand learning. The parents themselves should start primary education while the child is still at the preschool age, or pay a tutor. After elementary school, there must be difficult exams to progress to secondary schools and—supported by the state—a network of educational institutions, mainly private, to help students prepare for these exams.

Poland should be overwhelmed by the euphoria of learning because knowledge, when it is common and at a high level, ensures the security of a nation.

Before introducing a difficult and ambitious new program, all teachers should be examined to see whether they are able to implement such a program. Unfortunately, there will be no place in the school for teachers who do not meet or exceed the appropriate qualifications.

Education up to and including the matura exam should be

free, as providing education up to this level is the responsibility of the state. Students in primary schools should wear uniforms, which will make them proud to belong to a given school. At universities, I would recommend introducing low-cost student loans to pay for tuition fees. On the other hand, those who are capable and less wealthy should be supported by the state with scholarships.

As a general rule, no sharp mind can be wasted. And citizens, parents, and young people should be aware that toil not a little effort! Graduating from a good school with good results will pay off, giving one the chance for attractive employment.

The social prestige of the school, teaching, and education must grow!

Entering the details of the program, I consider it very important to saturate teaching with precise knowledge, especially regarding mathematics. At the same time, foreign languages should be taught, especially English, which is now the number-one international language. We should strive to make it a second language for every Pole. Hence, I believe that companies should organize intensive courses for those employees who, for some reason, have not mastered English at school.

On the other hand, students should not be overburdened with subjects that are of little use to the development of intelligence and technical thinking, which is, after all, the philosophical goal. Only people with high technical intelligence will understand the modern industrial world and will play significant roles in it. May the Poles be the most numerous among them.

This does not mean, of course, that one should neglect artistic objects, art history, and the like, as these things allow one to develop one's imagination and creative fantasy and thus also to contribute to the development of inventiveness.

The Church makes a huge contribution to moral education, and therefore, with the support of the government, it should participate in the implementation of the educational program. I believe that lessons on religion, ethics, and morality (one to two hours a week) should be compulsory. At the end of the year, a normal grade should be given, as for any other subject, that would contribute to promotion to the next class. I am however, opposed to teaching religion directly at school; I think catechetical rooms in parishes are a more appropriate place. Children of other faiths, or from families of nonbelievers, would have religion replaced by ethics. The curricula of these lessons should be coordinated by the church with the Ministry of Education. These lessons should be taken very seriously, as they should bring the foundations of morality and order to the country.

Outstanding world specialists in those fields where Poland does not have its own high level of specialists should be invited to lectures at Polish universities. I am thinking mainly of electronics and computer and programming specialists.

Graduating from a good university should automatically get one a good corporate or government job; however, admission to such a university must be limited by a strict examination. Government-sponsored private schools should specialize in exam preparation.

The times of laissez faire are history. Today the state, including the Polish one, must energetically support economic development. If the government is too weak for this because it does not have a parliamentary majority, the president must assume this role.

The cooperation between administration and business must be close and based on partnership. Frequent meetings and consultations with the participation of representatives of both parties should take place on an ongoing basis. The state must actively support the development of modern industry!

Of course, for the administration to meet this goal, its officials must be educated and intelligent. These are the administration employees that Polish education should provide, as I mentioned above.

In order to industrialize and modernize the country, an equivalent of the Japanese MYTHA should be established in Poland. The tasks of this organization would be as follows:

- offering advice, free consultations, and assistance for every industry department
- giving tax breaks for the purchase of new machinery and for investments
- offering advice and tax relief for export-oriented companies
- taking care of political relations with the countries to which the industry exports
- help in obtaining loans
- improving living conditions without slowing economic growth.
- organization of free but obligatory seminars for management staff to inculcate subordinates with the principles of modern capitalism
- industry development via low interest rates on profits in the initial period

However, all this cannot be achieved through direct administrative impact on business. An atmosphere of mutual trust and a common goal must arise. The following issues should be the topics of the seminars organized by the ministry:

I. People as the main factor of progress

- the role of quality control groups in implementing Deming's theory (about which I wrote more in the previous chapter)

- graduate employment policy (application of two criteria: knowledge and character)
- the purposefulness of conducting continual staff training in companies
- personnel policy in the field of promotions

    Promotions at workplaces will be awarded on the basis of years worked, education, attitudes, and relationships. At the management level, managerial and employee skills will be taken into account. The close connection of promotions, higher earnings, and the number of years worked will contribute to the formation of strong work teams. In general, everyone will be admitted to the lowest level, depending on his or her education. The emphasis should be on good companies hiring good students and specialists from good schools.

II. Workplaces as social environments

- taking care of the plant for the social matters of employees and creating an atmosphere conducive to the integration of all staff in the likeness of a family
- educational and social engineering qualifications of managerial staff
- allowing the staff to develop a sense of loyalty (which can be reduced to the issue of what a modern manager should be like in relation to employees)
- organization of joint social events outside working time as a method of consolidation and integration of personnel
- the role of middle management in developing plans and the direction of bottom-up decision-making (Deming's philosophy)
- the positive effect of intensive work on health (Statistics have shown that intensive work with good nutrition and

rest has a positive effect on longevity and reduces infant mortality, as can be seen in the case of the Swedes and the Japanese.)

- the role of trade unions—why they should be limited in their operation to one plant only

III. Awareness of development

- thinking in terms of long-term plans and understanding that production is a more important factor in development than profit and sales
- work ethic and interpersonal cooperation—the plant–employee relationship
- the ability to set a common goal for active groups (as not all can compete with all, meaning there must be a common denominator)
- Reduction of excessive stockpiling to avoid unnecessary investment and storage costs, "parts on time," following the introduction of Deming's theory

I see a further role of the state and the government in the establishment of Przemysłowy Bank Rozwojowy and Bank Eksport - Import. The government commission of professionals should decide on the allocation of loans. The government should guarantee loans for investments for those approved by the commission.

In my opinion, state-owned factories must not be closed down. The role of the government is to modernize them and then sell them to private hands.

As in the period of Japan's most prosperous development, the government should build modern factories. Once used for training purposes, they can then be privatized. Experts will be invited to the period of construction and adaptation of new technologies.

They will be well paid during the period necessary (as short as possible), provided that their skills are transferred and used.

Privatization and the sale of existing Polish plants should be carried out very carefully and, above all, in the hands of Polish companies.

It is important that the state supports the development of medium and small businesses in a special way. Let's not forget that these sectors account for as much as 99 percent of the entire world economy and provide the most jobs. At the time of development, start-up taxes should be very low.

The task of the government is to draw up a five-year plan together with business representatives, as well as a ten-year plan aimed at doubling the national income. The ten-year plan must include the following:

- improvement of infrastructure (telecommunications, roads, ports, airports, and so forth)
- Creation of tax preferences for the development of private housing
- provision of development stimuli for the heavy and chemical industries, especially in the areas of modern machines and devices applicable in other industries
- provision of development incentives to increase exports
- an increase in the professional knowledge of employees
- an increase in the number of research workers
- a reduction of the distance between traditional and modern industry and leveling of the differences in the economic development of individual regions of Poland

The administration also can and must make a significant contribution to changing the mentality of society in the approach to saving. Savings should be rewarded with tax breaks. Following the Japanese example, income from interest on bank deposits should

be exempt from tax. In the case of Poland, it is proposed to set this
threshold at PLN 50,000.

The government can and should counteract strikes, especially
long ones, which should be banned altogether. An impartial arbi-
tration board should intervene when employees and the employer
cannot reach a compromise.

The state power cannot hesitate to protect itself for the sake of
its own market. Excessive importation must be counteracted by a
system of customs and approvals. It would also be appropriate to
prohibit foreign companies from building businesses in Poland.
As a result, this will allow Polish companies to develop and improve quality production.

As of today, an important task of the government is to complete privatization and finally carry out reprivatization (i.e., return
nationalized property to its former owners). Control over the influence of money is no less important, as inflation may turn out
to be the bane of the young Polish capitalist economy.

There is a simple cause-and-effect relationship. Low economic
development leads to poverty and hence to crime, alcoholism,
drug addiction, prostitution, and other such issues. High economic growth, conversely, means prosperity and a reduction in
the scale of these plagues, and therefore leads to increased security. Of course, security should also be supervised by the army
and the police, which cannot run out of money, but first of all you
need to invest in industry!

Let's get a grip. We are a nation that has already achieved a lot
in history, and there is more it can do! I believe that, thanks to the
deliberate and concerted effort of several generations, Poland will
again become a power like the one it was in the times of Bolesław
the Brave, Casimir the Great, and the Jagiellonian!

CHAPTER 9

ON GOOD MANAGEMENT

★ ★ ★

It is sad to say that the economic governance system in force in most countries is outdated. Almost everywhere, the principle of transferring orders from top to bottom dominates, which reduces the bottom to the role of a thoughtless executor of orders. Psychologists point out that autocracy in enterprise management has a negative effect on the well-being of employees, worsens the atmosphere, and thus leads to lower productivity. After all, it is understandable that a person who does not like his job and company and who restricts all activity to fulfilling orders (or rather pretending to be following them) will not be a good employee! Performing tasks in a collective gives him pleasure. Such a person will be an efficient employee, bringing a clear benefit to both the enterprise and the entire economy.

But how to make employees like and feel good about their plants? The prescription for this was issued in 1950 by an American statistician, Dr. W. Edward Deming. The concept of quality developed in 1954 by Dr. J. M. Juran is based on his theory.

Characteristically, America was not really interested in
Deming's theory (maybe because it was too choked with military
and economic success after World War II), but it was adopted by
the Japanese. Today, the entire modern industry of Asia is managed according to his system, and the annual Deming Award is
one of the most prestigious in the field of factory management.

Only recently has the work of American scientists via Asia
returned to the USA, in the way of a modern management system with good results, as exemplified by IBM, TRW, 3M, Ford,
General Electric, Dana, Hewlett-Packard, Motorola, GM, and
many others. I will talk more about the implementation of the
Deming system in Ford plants in a moment, which will allow
the reader to better understand what the management system
is all about.

Already the first move of Dr. Deming displays his philosophy
well in this regard. During a personal meeting with the president
of Ford, he clearly emphasized that the condition for the successful implementation of the system was its approval by high officials
of the company.

In Japan, his system caught on with fifty major industry decision makers who attended the initial lectures. Ford agreed and,
hired as a consultant, Deming began working on management
awareness.

Dr. Deming taught that in human nature, regardless of culture or nationality, there is a rush toward self-improvement. A
company that wants to implement a modern management system
must understand that the human factor—people, simply put—is
more important than technology. You have to bet on people and
invest in them first!

The management must openly and honestly talk to the staff
about the company's condition, its goals, and its objectives. There
will be nothing wrong if one provides information of an accounting nature (not necessarily in full detail, of course). Management

needs to make clear the benefits of the five-year transition to the new system and gain the approval of trade unions and workers.

It is impossible to implement the system without removing the barrier of the worker–managers of the system. It must be made clear to people that the purpose of introducing innovation is not to cut costs, but to increase quality. It must be emphasized that if plants do not switch to modern management, they will never produce and sell their products on the global market. Everything about the new plans should be published in the company newspaper or newsletter.

A statement or even a manifesto containing declarations, principles, values, and guiding ideas that will guide the company from today on should be produced. Indicate that it is about quality improvement and that the people on the priority list are and will be ahead of the product and profit.

Here I am giving as an example just such a manifesto signed by Ford in 1994:

> Ford's mission. values and guiding ideas.
>
> MISSION: - " we must constantly improve the quality of our service products to satisfy the customer, allow us to operate successfully as a business and provide a reasonable return of profits for equity owners and business owners."
>
> VALUES: "How to reach our goal from the assumptions of the mission is as important as the mission itself. The fundamental success of our Department lies in three basic values.
>
> People - Our people are our power. They are the source of intelligence for our Corporation, they

are the source of the reputation and survival forces for the development of our plants. Everyone's active involvement and teamwork are at the core of our human values.

Products - Our product is the end result of our efforts and should be the best, serving customers all over the world. As our product is judged, we will also be judged.

Profit - Profit is the final measure of how efficiently we deliver customers the best product for their needs. Profit is needed to survive and thrive.

GUIDING RULES:

"Quality is the most important thing. In order to satisfy the customer, the quality of our products must be at the top of our list. "The customer is at the center of everything we do. We must strive for excellence in everything we do: in our products, in their safety and value, and in our service, in our human coexistence, in our competitiveness and profitability."

Employees commitment is our guiding idea. We are like a team. We must all treat others with trust and respect."

Sellers and suppliers are our partners. Our facilities must maintain healthy, positive relationships with vendors, suppliers, and business partners."

"Honesty and impartiality cannot be undermined. Our plants all over the world must operate

on the principles of fairness and impartiality with
a positive contribution to society. Our doors are
open to men and women without national bias or
personal beliefs."

One may say, "That is a beautiful declaration, but how are all these noble plans to be implemented?" Well, you just have to start with an honest, open discussion. Let everyone tell you what is wrong with the company and how to improve it. No one should fight criticism, because an employee who is afraid to criticize is also afraid of the company.

After breaking the ice, in the course of subsequent discussions, people will feel trust in each other and become more harmonious as a collective. This is a very big step toward improving production. In the next stage, the training of the production staff should be dealt with, and thus we come to the third Deming point, the so-called employee engagement.

Create groups of ten employees, including managers and masters, where all are treated equally and have equal voting rights. At the meetings of these groups, initially, once a week for an hour, allow each member to talk about his or her concerns about production and more. After a series of such meetings, employees will start to feel at ease, and the interpersonal atmosphere will improve.

The chairman, trained for group work, will start a discussion on the problems of the department. Such an exchange of views can be of colossal importance, because "every ten heads are better than one." Sometimes, even at such meetings, people find confirmation of their individual ideas, which under normal circumstances they would not even dare to express. The chairman may ask specific questions: "What can we do to improve the quality of our products?" or "Where is the waste in the plant?" If the discussion is going nowhere, it is a signal that the chairman probably needs to be changed.

Remember that an employee feels proud when asked what he thinks about a problem in the company. And this raising of his self-esteem has value in itself, even if what he said was not entirely accurate. However, where a group of intellectual involvement is liberated, a suggestion box is implemented, and brainstorming is provoked, there—on the basis of the interference of ideas and statistics—many legitimate ideas are born. And these bottom-up suggestions are then analyzed by the engineering staff and implemented. In this way, the company and the employees double, financially and mentally, as their self-esteem grows.

The bottom-up suggestion system seems to have three stages of development. In the beginning, it is the task of the management to make employees interested in the plant's problems and to make them express rationalizing opinions, no matter how primitive they may be. Later, employees are made aware of the need for additional training in order to make their opinions more professional. Only when employees have developed the habit of expressing their opinions and have adequate knowledge does the system really start to work. According to Deming, maturing to this state, and therefore seeing the economic fruit develop, takes five to ten years. All attempts to cut corners and artificially accelerate will fail!

There are many groups that operate throughout a plant in all departments. In each group, someone has to keep a record of the number of suggestions made and the money saved as a result of each. Each group's success must be publicized throughout the company. There is no point in comparing the groups in terms of their performance, as this could kill the "free spirit" of the enterprise.

Familiarize the entire production staff with how to use statistical control methods to improve product quality and production processes. Emphasize the need for all staff to make uninterrupted efforts to continuously improve quality.

A consultant should be employed to train production staff in statistical quality control, and a psychologist specialized in group work issues should be brought on board. Local universities can provide this kind of specialist. The transition to the new system will absolutely pay off. By using statistics, it is possible to precisely determine where the errors are and thus improve the production system.

Often, high quality is associated with luxury, which is not always true. After all, cheap products should also be of high quality; every buyer will subscribe to this statement. It is a problem getting the producers to have the same opinion, and unfortunately one sees too much tolerance in regard to one's own products, especially when the manufactured thing is not the end product. That is why it is useful to popularize this statement: "Are you proud enough of your own products to buy them yourself?"

How does the statistical control mechanism work? If the quality of the products is bad, 80 percent of it is a system or process fault. A quality discrepancy is often seen in factory production—a good product comes off the belt one minute, a defect the next. Therefore, control points and test points must be established throughout the entire production process.

Take, for example, refining the properties of a metal by immersing it in hot oil. For the process to run properly, the oil must be at a certain temperature, which depends on its amount and the amount of gas burned to heat it. These measurements are the control points for workers. They watch the gauges, adjust the valves, and thus get the right result. For their supervisor, these are checkpoints (i.e., he checks the work of the subordinates, possibly giving them tips on how to regulate the amounts of gas and oil). The point of control, for the supervisor, is measurement of the final oil temperature, which has a direct impact on the result.

It is known that all works in a plant overlap, or are dependent on each other. Here I am talking about the so-called Deming's circle (i.e., continuous cooperation between the research, design, production, and sales departments). Without this, it is impossible to achieve the main goal of satisfying the customer. Each employee runs his own control graph, marking some values on the ordinate, others on the abscissa. Two horizontal lines are limiting, and any control point outside the range is an alarm signal.

When such abnormal points begin to appear on the graph, the worker goes back to the source of their origin and immediately eliminates the error. At Ford, assembly line workers are so trusted that they can stop the entire line to eliminate the error.

The control and checking points, combined into a system covering all employees in each department and production level, are called total quality control (TKJ).

TKJ also operates on the top floors of the company, where managers of equal rank establish mutual control points over each other (i.e., the intersections of managerial functions). The method of such an intersection is decided by the top management of the plant or a committee of about ten decision makers with a chairman appointed by the director himself. In terms of importance, such a commission is second only to the board of directors of the corporation. It is this commission that, at its meetings, defines the company's goals and ways to achieve them, and plans production and sales.

For the system to run smoothly, each manager needs to know exactly which checkpoints and checks are his. His checkpoints are his subordinates' checkpoints, as I wrote about above. It takes a lot of training and discipline to successfully apply statistical quality control.

This system eliminates traditional bureaucratic and staff-based control inspectors. It is a more efficient and effective method. It allows errors to be spotted faster and reduces waste. Above all, it increases the employees' self-esteem, their morale, and their degree of personal involvement in the company's affairs.

Twice a year, the company's president checks how the TKJ is

working. As a rule, half a day with the management and another half a day with the workers is enough for this. The president checks how the statistical charts work in practice.

However, the condition for the implementation of TKJ is the earlier development of standards. Without the standards of machines, employees, and management, the introduction of the new system is unthinkable. Of course, it is not enough just to set standards; people must also be trained to comply with them.

Expand the definition of "quality" and apply this quality to your products so that they amaze and delight the customer. Engage with customers by asking about negative comments and the reasons they prefer a competitor's products. Encourage employees to constantly think about improving the quality of products.

Try to create an atmosphere between the departments cooperating within the company so that they treat each other as customers and constantly increase the quality of products among themselves.

Pay a visit to your competitors and see why they do it better. Ford was sending hundreds of people to Japan when switching to modern management to visit the Mazda and Toyota factories. The Americans enviously watched the Japanese productivity. They were particularly impressed with the ongoing method of sourcing production, eliminating costly inventory, and warehousing. "It's hard to increase your sales by 10%," explained one director, "but you can cut costs by 10%."

The confrontation of the two automotive powers was a shock for Ford. Of the nearly one hundred people he sent to Japan, no one, on his return, was able to point to any area of American superiority, but everyone saw the advantage of the Japanese in many areas. A myth had collapsed, as up to that point the Americans had explained Japan's economic successes with government protectionism and modern technology. Now it had become clear that it was based on management and organization. The grain of thought of Dr. Deming had resulted in a harvest in Japan, not in America, which did not even want to hear about these theories.

This experience provided strong reason for Ford to also switch his own company to the new management system. The fact is that in the past, Japanese industry absorbed foreign technologies and achieved high productivity and product quality. Now it is focused on flexible factory technology, which means that it has the ability to quickly adapt the production of a new product according to customer and market requirements.

There is no doubt that there is a global demand for new technologies. The most important thing is what happens after the discovery of new technology. Initially the product is expensive and not of the best quality. And here efforts should be focused on lowering the cost of mass production, and improving the product and its quality. And for all this, a modern management system is necessary. So-called management participation is the core of the entire system of modern management.

It's worth noting that in most companies around the world, management doesn't like risk. This is due to the system that was more restrictive toward the perpetrators of failures which were more easily tangible than those resulting from discouraging actions, the latter of which were more difficult to notice and calculate. The rule of bureaucracy and the vertical direction of directives also discourage risk. It is enough to follow the boss's order (or simulate execution) to have your money and peace of mind.

In order to change this mentality, the implementation of the new management system must be started with successive training of main management and middle management, and this must involve the innovative science of workers. Dr. Deming attaches great importance to staff training; he recommends five-day courses in statistical quality control and group work, as well as, for managers and directors, additional three-day management courses. After this comes six weeks of practical activities, and then two days for discussion and general theoretical repetition of the problem.

The point is to make decision-making not about the result, but about the process. Each activity performed in the factory is a process that needs to be constantly improved.

The features that this leadership should have are discipline, managerial time, willingness to develop and learn, active participation and inclusion, morality, and ease of communication with others.

In order to create process-oriented leadership in the new system, every senior plant official must complete a compulsory course. Some executives will not like the new system because they will think it takes away their absolute power. Management participation is simply an operating style in which subordinates have the opportunity to say what they think and in which their ideas are incorporated into the final decision-making process.

The "committed employees" system is going to be nourishing the "management stake." Here is what principals and managers will be taught in their courses.

After reading the betting declaration with goals and values, higher officials will spend 50 to 80 percent of their time trying to convey the idea of modern management to their subordinates. They all need to know how important people are, and they must respect every employee in the plant. They all need to know that an educated and qualified employee is the only defense against strong competition. Products and technologies can be bought, but usually that will not be enough without the support of people. In their moves, they will replace stringent regulations and trust checks. Their slogan will be "We trust our people."

The word "customer" will be placed on a pedestal. Here, as an example, I will mention that there was a rule introduced by the American factories of IBM. In those factories, employees were dismissed from their jobs if they received a phone call from a customer and the phone rang more than twice.

Create collaborative groups across departments to improve key products and plant services. Eliminate people's vertical, bureaucratic dependence. With fewer degrees of vertical dependence among people, there will be less chance of making a mistake, and more authority will be given to people at lower levels. There are only three vertical layers at the leading American factory Dana: the workers, their managers, and the factory director.

The emphasis is on interpersonal understanding being open, free, and face-to-face.

When promoting management, the opinions of subordinates are taken into account. A follower of group work is promoted faster than an individual. It is easy to see who can work with people or sit down with them and discuss problems or put the group goal above their personal goal. Directors and managers must get down to the ground and treat everyone equally and with respect.

As the modern plant management system advances, senior officials and workers receive higher-level training. Directors and managers must be in the habit of asking their subordinates, "What do you think about this?"

Ford found that European managers rarely communicated with US executives prior to the "management share" rates and that these rates were followed by frequent exchanges of views and insights on what they thought that I, as chairman of the establishments, should do for them. But during the second two-day course, everyone said what he or she had done and asked if he or she was on the right track.

Facilities that wish to emphasize the importance of employee engagement and management involvement will organize them around the key product they are currently working on. Such a key product for Ford, when the company switched to the modern management system, was the Taurus. For Ford, the Taurus has become a child of the new system and the number-one car sold in the US for the last nine years. It was a confirmation that the modern management system and group work are effective. The rank and file working on development of the new Taurus car were given more freedom in making decisions.

The groups behind this car purchased the fifty best-designed midsize cars from all over the world. They took them apart and studied how their components were designed and manufactured. After months of research, the group decided which improvements were to be made to the Taurus. The entire program of the Taurus project lasted six years from start to finish. It takes four years for a new car, with a new engine and gearbox, to be developed by Toyota or Honda

After the complete implementation of the new management system, sometimes within in a few months or sometimes several years, one can feel changes for the better in the quality of products and in service. This period depends on the size of the venture and from what point it started, but at some point, this progress will naturally slow down. This will be a second phase, during which it will be time to test new technologies and the ways the factory and offices have been designed. It will be the most difficult period, in which all employees—most importantly the engineering team behind the plants, will participate. Old professionals, veterans, are a great source of information because they know best how existing systems work. The plants that constantly introduce new methods of production are the plants of the future.

It must not be forgotten that if plants are doing good business, then employees are provided with jobs and receive higher salaries. The goal of the venture should be not only short-term profits but also a profitable existence in the long run. It is important that everyone benefits from the higher profits, not just the senior plant officials. Praise and public praise are also very important, especially for top workers. Managers should never publicly criticize people for minor mistakes or other misconduct.

Money spent on the latest technology is money well invested, while automation does not always bring the intended perfect result. In the 1970s and early 1980s, Toyota and Nissan invested in two other directions. Nissan has invested huge sums of money in automating its factories and has eliminated a lot of work. Toyota, on the other hand, invested in people, training them professionally and getting them to engage in teamwork. If you want to see a factory that is still operating after the lights go out and everyone goes home, Nissan is the place you should look to. But if you want to see a factory where everything works like clockwork, then Toyota is the place you should focus on. Toyota employs quite a lot of people and uses machines that are not always of the newest type. This is a rather conservative approach regarding automation, and it was a smart move to bet on people. Toyota is a high-performance factory, produces high-quality cars, and is very profitable.

As you can see, people are the most important. Potential leaders must be deployed to all sorts of factory assignments in order for them to grow and demonstrate. Dr. Deming said that three characteristics characterize a person who has the potential to become a leader in any organization: his position and status, his messages, and his personality. The first is hard to control and will not change until people are promoted or demoted. On the other hand, people can work on the other two if they get the chance to develop in the organization and serve customers better.

All officials in the Ford company conduct interviews at certain universities and colleges to hire new people. When interviewing potential candidates, officials look at their academic progress and ask whether they are team players. Have the parties been active in university organizations or in the environment where they live? What are their characters, attitudes, and behaviors in various situations? Are they confident? Have they been members of clubs or played for sports teams? Do they have the drive to discover, and are they curious about new things?

At Ford, the modern management system first began to develop in Europe. There, Ford employees felt comfortable working in groups, and at this point, Ford plants in Europe are leading the Ford plants in the USA in group work on new products. Ford plants and other American companies that have a modern management system are able to produce a new product faster and more efficiently.

European Ford in the UK has had difficulty installing a modern management system in its industry. The main reason for this was a large number of different unions in each plant fighting for power. Workers went on strikes or interrupted production on any pretext without any consequences. Currently, eight UK Ford factories practice modern management systems without the general support of the workers.

In Germany, things took a completely different turn at Ford. After the Second World War, relations between the management and German workers grew stronger, and government regulations were also drawn up stating that representatives of plant workers must sit on the corporate board. All German workers and the lower management belong to the workers' boards, or unions. The head of these unions sit on the corporate board. The corporate board has the right to vote over any employee training, even if the unions are against it. In order to also gain support from the unions, union representatives were invited to Ford USA for a ten-day training visit. After this visit, union representatives fully endorsed the modern management system. Today, all Ford factories in Germany operate fully under the new management system, which has significantly improved the quality of Ford products.

Sometimes it happens that after the introduction of a modern management system, supervisors may be stuck in place, not knowing what to do next. There are a few questions they must ask themselves: Do all employees really understand this system? Do they really know what the terms "committed employees" and "management involvement" mean? This is not rocket science, but it requires a lot of repetition. If the speaker communicates the concept to the workers while handing out brochures and that's it, that's not enough.

Employees must hear about they system from their immediate supervisors not once, but many times, and the process must be repeated. Shifting an employee who does not want to work in the group to another job will give a strong signal that the establishment supports the introduction of the new system.

If a manager is unable to involve employees in the new management system, it is probably his fault, not the fault of the employees. Managers have to try to get everyone involved in the system, but if a third of the workers in the factories get on board, the rest will follow.

After the modern management system is fully implemented and adopted in the plant, employees will enjoy the new working conditions so much that they will not want to go back to the old system.

With group work in mind, we need to change the way we raise our children. Children, from an early age, are geared to compete against one another. If the youth at school work together, we consider them to be cheating. Students graduate from high school or university, where they are required to work individually all the time, but at work they are required to work collectively. This should be changed, with children being taught to work in small groups from a very early age.

The topic I write about in this chapter is extremely serious in today's world of fierce market competition, and for many countries, it means the difference between success and failure. In this short chapter, I do not answer many practical questions related to modern management systems, but I wanted to present this topic to the reader.

I am not writing about seven statistical tools—charts that are used to improve the quality of products. Likewise, I am not writing about the annual Deming Award and its criteria for the establishment of the best quality control system and many other aspects of this philosophy.

My book *The Managerial Philosophy that Builds a Strong Poland* (which every business manager should know) is devoted to a completely modern management system.

I wish that all Polish plants would gradually switch to a modern management system. The president and the government must help the plants compete on the international stage. All existing laws and regulations must be checked in terms of their impact on the competitiveness of Polish plants.

CHAPTER 10

KAZIA

★ ★ ★

Kazia recorded the story of her life on three cassette tapes. She does not use the first person, but speaks about a protagonist, as if she wanted to keep a greater distance from events, or maybe more anonymity.

She was born in the workers' Wola district. It grew—in an exotic way from today's perspective—as a landscape of tenement houses, small workshops, and shops. There existed her house in Płocka, the yard where Polish and Jewish children played, the school of the Felician Sisters for Mermaids, where she studied.

And in Wola was a great deal of trade, which she took up when she was ten years old. She helped her father sell toys in Kercelego Square. She was the daughter of a Warsaw merchant. Handel shaped her, hardened her, and was a faculty and a way of life.

In her world, her Warsaw, Hitler and Stalin declared war. The first destroyed the city's body with fire and iron, and then they struck its soul.

But a handful of people like Kazia, like survivors from a sunken ship, endured and continued to do their jobs. It was thanks to them that in the worst occupation or PRL crisis it was possible to buy "cardless" meat, better clothes, and shoes without official assignment. In the darkest moments for the country, these people were the last living tissue of the economy being murdered by the enemy. Unfortunately, no monuments are erected for such merits in Poland, yet still some compatriots repeat nonsense about the black market and speculators, following the German and Communist propaganda.

Kazia was an ordinary, optimistic, honest Varsovian, brave and resourceful in the most difficult situations. She knew Warsaw during the twenty years it was under occupation, as well as the Warsaw that was raised from ruins to real socialism, which she did not want to, and could not, submit herself to, as it was too alien to her honest and enterprising nature.

During the uprising in the last period of the war, she was taken to Germany, where she spent time in a labor camp. Under American bombing, in a basement with broken windows, I was born on a frosty at the beginning of March 1945. She had to go to great lengths to ensure that the baby and she would have at least a minimum subsistence. She mentioned that there was a Polish woman who abandoned her baby, unable to cope. But she survived.

Then she spent years in the States. In her sixties, she passed the exam and became an American citizen to help her daughter emigrate. I find it hard to contain a smile when I hear in her story that "almost did not pass out" or "she wanted to go outside."

Were it not for her, I do not know whether I would have made my way in America. I owe my success to a great extent to her self-sacrificing presence with me.

When Poland regained independence and freed itself from the absurd system, she decided to return, and after years of forced separation, she began to do her job—trading—again. And, by the way, she wanted to once again help her son.

Looking at her activity, diligence, and the enormity of effort she made, it seems incredible that she was already over seventy years old. But she had that nature always, until the tragic day a warehouse fire interrupted her busy life.

Courageous, wise, and enterprising Kazia—my beloved mother.

CHAPTER 11

UKRAINE

★ ★ ★

W hat is the history of Ukraine? Why was Ukraine never an independent country prior to the collapse of the Union of Soviet Socialist Republics (USSR)?

Ukraine was a part of Poland for five hundred years. At the end of the seventeenth century, there was a rebellion of Ukrainian Cossacks and Tatars led by Bohdan Khmelnytskyi. At that time, the king in Poland was Jan Kazimierz. Ukrainian rebels attacked and robbed castles and cities. King Jan Kazimierz called a "popular uprising" to suppress the Ukrainian rebellion. The popular uprising was one of the "Golden Freedoms" that later led to dismantling of Poland by Russia, Prussia, and Austria. Poland was erased from maps for 130 years.

The king could not have an army. Only during times of danger could the king call for a popular uprising, and the Polish nobility were obligated to appear with subordinates to fight in defense of the country.

After few days of fighting Ukrainian butchers, the army of King Jan Kazimierz, composed of the Polish nobility, began to rebel. They had had enough of war and wanted to return home.

Bohdan Khmelnytskyi introduced himself as a peasant and drunkard but turned out to be a clever politician. He was in correspondence with Moscow and wanted to join Ukraine to Tsarist Russia instead of preferring independence, and so it happened.

The Russians later expelled the Ukrainian Tatars, who inhabited Crimea and annexed Crimea to Russia. In 1956 Khrushchev transferred Crimea to Ukraine.

Ukraine is the largest European country with rich, arable land. However, under Stalin's rule, three million Ukrainians died of starvation. After the collapse of the USSR, President Putin said that was the greatest historical tragedy and never recognized Ukraine as an independent country.

The consequence of this is the Russian attack and today's war in Ukraine, which we cannot predict the outcome of. Putin took advantage of the US having a weak president.

Ukraine may become a member of the European Union, but it will not be admitted to NATO, because that could trigger a world war. Ukraine could join Poland again and solve two problems, but this would require (1) a referendum of the Ukrainian people and (2) the consent of the Polish government. History likes to repeat itself sometimes.

To protect Europe and America from Eastern foreign aggression, a plan should be implemented. As part of this plan, the following steps should be taken:

1. Rockets with nuclear warheads should be installed on Polish soil near Ukraine.
2. Poland should draft a free trade agreement with America to strengthen its economy.
3. Poland should buy American nuclear power stations from America.

04093268-00841307

Printed in the United States
by Baker & Taylor Publisher Services